They liked me, the horses, straightaway

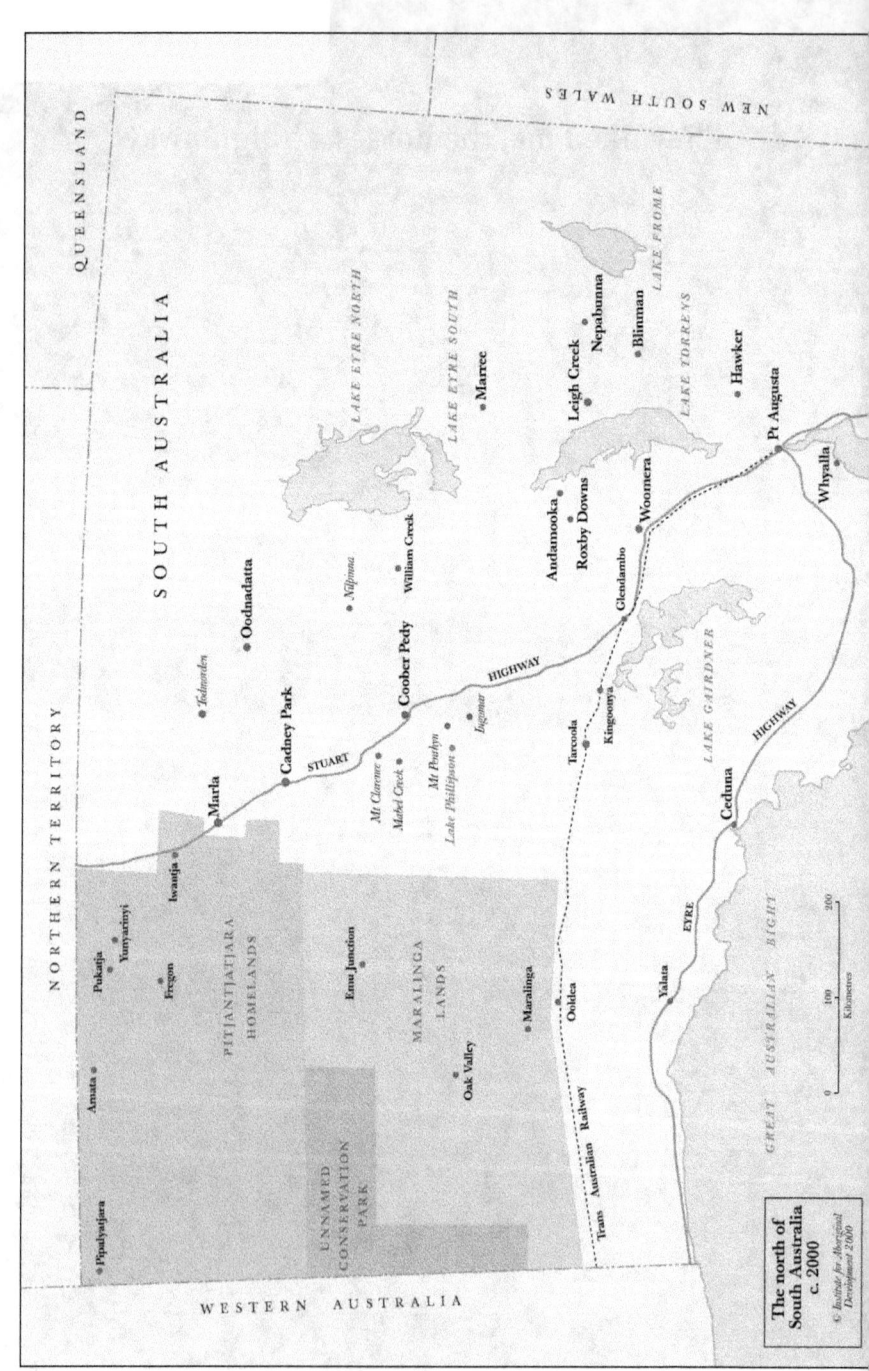

♦Marty Dodd♦

They liked me, the horses, straightaway

I dedicate this book
to my grandchildren and great-grandchildren.
M.D.

Acknowledgements

It was Mindy David Crombie who first suggested to Michele Madigan that she work with Marty Dodd to record his racehorse career.

For the initial funding of this project and for later assistance to ensure its publication, thanks are due to the Josephite Congregation.

Thanks to Christel Hauri, Christobel Mattingley, Ian Rankin, Rosie Dodd, Ljubica Markovic and others for their help.

Thanks to all who provided photographs, in particular to Faith Thomas (née Coulthard), Marie Nourse (née O'Leary) and the Traeger family.

Thanks to Stephen Matthews of Ginninderra Press for his part in the publication of this important Australian story.

They liked me, the horses, straightaway…
ISBN 978 1 74027 067 0
Copyright © text Marty Dodd 2000
Copyright © cover drawing John Fang 2000
Copyright © illustrations as indicated
Frontispiece map used by kind permisssion of IAD Press

First published 2000
Reprinted 2017

GINNINDERRA PRESS
PO Box 3461 Port Adelaide 5015 Australia
www.ginninderrapress.com.au

◆Contents◆

Prologue	7
Earliest Days	9
Taken Away	10
The Father	12
Life in the Home	14
Three Brothers and the Baby	17
Life at Mabel Creek	19
The 1939 Flood	21
Changing Over to Cattle	23
They Liked Me, the Horses…	25
The Station Hands at Mabel Creek	27
Stock Work, Mustering	28
The Americans	30
Leaving Mabel Creek	32
Life at Ingomar	34
Battle Axe at the Kingoonya Races	35
The Kingoonya Cup…	37
…and the Oodnadatta Cup	38
Mustering the Sheep	43
The Changeover to Motorbikes	44
The Main Musterer	46
Finding the Father Again	49
The Father Passes Away	51

The Medal from the Queen	53
Married Life	55
Over on the West Coast	57
Andamooka	59
Giving the Opal a Try	60
Opal… Ohhh!	62
Making a Claim	64
Selling the Opal	66
The Bomb!	68
Moving to Coober Pedy For Good	71
The Bulldozers in Full Swing	74
Drills and Blowers on the Field	77
Bringing Up the Kids	79
I Know the Area That Much	83
Epilogue	87
Appendix 1 Timeline	89
Appendix 2 From the *Australian Dictionary of Biography*	90
Appendix 3 From *The Adelaide Chronicle*, 1956	92
Appendix 4 British Nuclear Bomb Testing in SA 1953–1963	93

◆Prologue◆

I was breaking them horses in and, before I left Mabel Creek, I went from there with a mob of horses to Kingoonya to try some of them out – to see how they'd go at the Kingoonya Races. We used to have the races about Easter time every year.

In those days, you know, the Aboriginal lads wasn't allowed to ride horses – I supposed they reckoned we weren't good enough for them blokes. But I just took it in my stride – didn't worry. I'm just what I am, wouldn't try to change my ways. (They accepted me at Mabel Creek and Ingomar and all those places – I could sit at their table.)

Well, we went to the races and the first oldest horse I had, I called him Tommyhawk. I was using him for a stock horse all the time at the station, mustering bullocks and all that sort of thing. And so we took him to the races and he was only a young horse about three-year-old then, that Tommyhawk, that first time.

We was ready for the race and I said, 'I'm not putting my horse in the race.'

They had a race, what they called a Black Boys' Race, at the end of the day.

'I'm putting my horse in the Black Boys' Race,' I said, and I was going to ride him myself.

'No, you're a bit heavy,' my old boss, Alf Turner, said.

So we put this young bloke on, named Archie Lang. He was only a young kid then. He was my best mate.

'Yeah,' I said. 'We'll let him ride. He's a lightweight – he's only about five or six stone or something.' Told him, 'Let him have his head when he comes around the straight.'

So he jumped on the horse. Tommyhawk was a quiet horse – never jumped around. When they lined up for the race, he's just standing there, standing quiet. He'd just think he was just going out for an ordinary day's work. He could easily have pulled away from the little kid if he wanted to.

The race started and away they went!

Oh, I'm looking for that little bloke coming… Oh, there's that white-faced horse coming around the corner! And he come around that corner, coming into the straight. I could see that white face starting to stick out in the front. He come right round them 'cause he couldn't get through the middle. Takes that big a stride, that horse, he just shot straight past them! By the time he got into the straight, he was about forty yards in the front when he won the race! He had that lightweight – flat out he galloped!

He got the biggest shock, that little bloke, Archie Lang! Happy he was and pulled the horse up easy. That horse was a quiet horse – some racehorses are hard to pull up. He was well trained too – you just talk to him and just pull up. He won that race no worry at all!

Yes, that was the last race of the day. I wouldn't put my horse in their race – and they found out he was better than all them others that were galloping there, the way he won that race. I got interested in the horses after that.

◆ Earliest Days ◆

I'm not sure, but I think I was born at Todmorden – Todmorden Station out from Oodnadatta. I can't remember my mother. Mother was born between Pipalytjatjara and Coffin Hill. You can go straight south towards Ooldea way from there, but she never went that Ooldea way.

She passed away when I was four or five years old. I don't remember her, her face – too young to know her properly. I had my aunty looking after me there. She was Angelina Scobie's mother, my mother's cousin. I didn't hardly know my mother. Angelina's mother used to look after me because I was a small little one running around. She's the one that used to be my nursemaid. She was round about sixteen, seventeen then, my aunty. (I didn't know who it was till I came back after the time in the Home. I was saying that, long ago, I only used to know one person in Todmorden country. And I was talking to this person – and that was Angelina's mother! She said, 'Oh, that was me looking after you!')

My mother was busy looking after the other little ones, I suppose – and the boys run around. But I must have been the pet for my aunty. See, I was with her most of the time when she'd go out hunting. We used to go out for goannas and rabbits. Sometimes there might be a big perentie around there, round Todmorden country. There're no *kaltas* – sleepy lizards – up there. She'd take me all the time, carry me around everywhere – I was spoilt, I think.

◆Taken Away◆

But I was with my mother when her youngest son was born – Stephen, that's the one. She passed away after that. I don't know much about that time when I was little. I got sent away to the Home when I was too little to know much.

Yes, it was from Todmorden that I went – she took the three of us to Oodnadatta, because that was before Stephen was born; my mother was expecting him. The father couldn't go with us, leave his work; he was one of the head stockmen at Todmorden. The mother, she was in the Oodnadatta hospital just about passing away then. 'Cause in those days, after birth, the woman had a lot of trouble. She might have lost a lot of blood – something like that.

Mr Green took us then. He came and picked us up when the mother died, took us away – the family of us boys. Yes, Mr Green – I think he was a missionary bloke, the same one that went to Ooldea later on. He came and took us from the camp in Oodnadatta. I had my aunties and all my relations looking after me in the camp – in the area where the police station is now. That's where we got taken away all together, from there. That was the time they were taking everybody away. Oh, they thought they were doing the right thing. I don't know what.

We stopped in the little mission home at Oodnadatta for about a week before we went down south, till my little baby brother, Stephen, could travel in the basket. We went straight into the Quorn home from living in Oodnadatta in the town.

There were three brothers when we went there – me and my two older brothers – and there was a baby; that was Stephen. He went down to the Home in a little basket, he was that small. Mr Green and we were feeding him the milk on the way down. I was about four or five – only young. I don't know much about it. We never went back to our own mothers and fathers. No.

They just took us. He wanted us; the father wanted us. In those days, no people was drinking. They were on reserves or in the station country. The parents and even the relations love you just the same – they love you. Doesn't matter who the father is – we're still the mother's child; they still want you.

◆The Father◆

Father came from the Northern Territory, way up. He's been all around the places – everywhere; all over the west side – the western region of South Australia – all over that area. He'd been to Docker River – it's straight on line from Ayers Rock, Uluru, to the boundary – inside the Northern Territory.

Close to Docker River is Katakutjara; it means two heads. (Kata Tjuta, the Olgas – that means many heads – is another place north of Uluru.) There's two hills there – Katakutjara; a dreamtime story those two hills are – where people used to travel in their dreams. My father, he's been working around there too – he made a lot of roads around there, around Docker River, in the old days.

When I went to the Old Age Home, when they were opening the Old Age Home there in 1995, the first bloke I talked to at Docker River knew my father. In fact, he took me out to show me the roads that my father and *his* father was making long ago. Oh, that bloke was only a little kid then. I was happy to find out that my relation was way out there too. His working life, I suppose. They never mentioned my mother's name. The old bloke's name – my old father – was Tommy Dodd. He was well known all over the country. (Not the other old bloke named Tommy Dodd, who went down to Yalata. He took his name after my father, because my father half grew him up there. He used to come down here, to Coober Pedy – staying here for a while. Just before that Bomb went off, I think. Then he took off from Coober Pedy down to Yalata way.)

My father, he came through from somewhere up the Top End – the other side of Tennant Creek. He came down here south, just travelling through with buggies. He was a worker – he worked for the stations. The first place I know where he was, was Henbury Station, alongside the Finke River. That station is right there where the Finke River Crossing is when you're going to Alice Springs. That's only just off the main highway. He was working there first, working his way down south.

Then he came to South Australia – probably travelled with a horse and buggy or camel. He had camels. Oh, when I last seen him, he had a camel with a sort of little cart with four wheels on it – with car wheels, rubber tyres.

When I left the Home and went out to work, I went to Mabel Creek. But my father was working in that area, years ago, breaking a mob of horses for Jim Robb, who owned all the horses. Jim Robb was really the owner of Granite Downs station, to the west of Oodnadatta. But it must have got a bit dry one year at Granite Downs, so they came down to Mabel Creek to the big waterhole where there was plenty of feed for the horses. He was breaking horses for Indian remounts, for the army. They send them away to India or somewhere. They might have a lot of horses riding and then they have to change the horses over. Must have been for the 1914 Great War. They only had horses in Granite Downs – that's where the army got the horses. They needed the mounted cavalry.

My father told me that when I was younger. My father was there, round Mabel Creek, years before Alf Turner or anybody else was there starting up the station. Mabel Creek was the first station that was started up west of Coober Pedy that had buildings. A shed – that's all it was. It was on the flat from the creek. (Later, when the flood came, it just washed away and they had to make up the station house on the side of the hill.)

Then, when my father came down towards Oodnadatta area, I think he met my mother. He might have married her at Mount Lindsay – Mount Lindsay west of Fregon – because that's my mother's country. 'Cause he was used to that country too. That's not far – just about 200 kilometres west from Amata, in the Pitjantjatjara lands, close to Mount Davies (Pipalyatjara), near the Western Australia border. That's where my homelands is.

♦ Life in the Home ♦

When I first went to Colebrook, Colebrook Home was about a mile out of Quorn. And later in years, they shifted further out from town – about two mile out. I went out there to the new place. I was one of the kids that used to run errands some of the time, and especially in the morning to go and get the mail. So I used to go before school starts and be back home for breakfast and go to school with the rest of the kids. All the kids mixed together – very good, those kids from in the town. We were all in the same classrooms – it didn't matter; we was all right.

On the weekends, the kids used to come home and they used to play around home then. No one used to go out much. Only I was in the habit of walking away. Sometimes I might come back dinner time, sometimes I mightn't even come back at all until supper time! I'd forget – I'd be walking around that long! Just all round, following the creeks about – and eating that gums off some of the trees – cassia bushes, they call them. I used to love that gums on the trees. It's something like chewing gum – and sweet.

They didn't even know I was missing. You know, I'd just walk away quietly and down to the creek about a mile away and walk around. All the other boys'd be playing around, doing other things back at home. I used to like walking around looking at the birds and see a few nests where there might be little eggs in them. I wouldn't touch it – just leave it, just have a look at it.

We had two ladies most of the time in charge of us. One was Sister Rutter and the main one was matron – Sister Hyde; she was the boss. Sometimes we'd have another young person there for a while too. But those two was the main ones. They used to stop there all the time looking after us kids. They were very good – kind with us. Because they were Christian ladies. They were really good people.

I used to think about my Dad a lot. But most of the time I'd forget, you know, because I'm playing round with all the kids. They had about thirty-two or thirty-three kids altogether there in the Home. Syd Waye; and that Loie – Lois O'Donoghue, you know, you hear a lot about her in the news; and the young one that was there – she come there as a bit of a baby from Nepabunna – Faith Coulthard. She's Faith Thomas now. She lives there most of the time now in the Home what's there – down at Quorn. She's the caretaker of Colebrook Home these days. Yes, she was a little baby when she first come there. We used to all nurse her.

Most of them were my relations – from all this end here, Oodnadatta way and Ernabella and all round them places. Some come from other places. Some of the Richards, Rita and Ricky, they come from down that way – round Quorn. And a few come from the Northern Territory – some of the Hayeses, two of the Hayes girls (Ada was one of them) and a boy, Freddie; three of them altogether. Parker O'Donoghue, he was the crippled bloke.

We all used to work. The boys used to work there till about thirteen or fourteen – then they ready to go out, when they finished school. We used to help all the time. I used to be one that's cutting the wood for the kitchen wood box. I'd keep filling that every day. And Saturdays, that'd be six armfuls. I'd used to take an armful at a time; put about six armfuls in and that'd last for the weekend.

They'd got to cook a lot of meals. They'd make stews. The bigger girls that'd not finished school a little bit, they used to cook around there. And some of the Home girls that were bigger – when they knocked off work, they were living around there looking after smaller kids. That was when the big girls had finished schooling, you know, some of them was living there. They were the ones that used to do the cooking.

Yes, I used to remember all those girls. We was all good friends. I don't think we had any trouble with the kids – we was all friendly together. No arguments, nothing at all. It might have been through the kind matron and sister we had. I think that we were all a happy family. It might have been through that. Yes, when we was in the Home, we was like brothers and sisters. All one big family.

Some of the girls kept in contact with me but the boys went their way. I've seen George Tongerie more than anybody. Julie van Horen's uncle just passed away lately – at Marree or Quorn. He was staying in the Home; Bruce Fielding was his name. I'm not much older than Lois O'Donoghue. I think Aileen was about my age – Aileen O'Donoghue and Clara Coulthard (used to be Brady). Emily Lester was just a bit older. She was one of the big girls. I tried to see Mona Paul in Alice Springs when I was up that way – I went a couple of times to find her place but missed out where the house was. She passed away not long after that.

I went up to grade six in the Home. I was about fourteen when they sent me out there – up this way – to Mabel Creek. Some of the those station blokes from up this way would just look around for a bloke. They came down for us – they got word that some of the boys were getting bigger – about fourteen years old. Alf Turner from Mabel Creek came right down to Colebrook Home. He offered to take us two boys, Syd Waye and me. He came down there to pick us up in his little old bomb – one of those little old cars, a little Essex, I think. He took Syd the first year. Then the year after that, he picked me up. We knew he was coming down. He must have rung up or wrote a letter about it. We was waiting for him to turn up.

✦Three Brothers and the Baby✦

The oldest brother passed away. He died in the Home in Quorn not long after he got there. He died from the ordinary flu. He was used to hot places. It was too cold for him. He's buried in the Quorn cemetery. I was only about six or seven.

And then, years after that, my other brother died there, around Quorn. He was the one who was crippled. He used to ride a bike around all the time. But see, he'd done something with his hip when he was a young lad – when he was a kid at Todmorden Station. They reckon he fell off the stockyard rails and got hurt. And see, they never sent him away to the hospital. They just kept him there at the station. You know, years ago, they never had any respect for Aboriginals much. They wouldn't have worried. 'Oh, he's only a little black kid.' Oh, he must have been in pain!

I stayed in the Home till I was about thirteen or fourteen. I don't know my exact right date, because you don't know it when you're born in the bush – but I put it down like that. When we were sent away to work, we were sent wherever they wanted to send us. Not to my father where he was.

And when Andy, the crippled one, came out of the Home, they sent him towards Copley – Nepabunna, round there – and Stephen was still in the Home at Quorn. After I came out of the Home, they sent Stephen down to Eden Hills and we sort of got separated. We were a long way apart, that's why we don't worry about one another today. I left Colebrook Home when he was only about six or seven and that's where we drifted apart – because I didn't go back. I was working all the time – never had any holidays. I stayed up this way, at Mabel Creek.

Only the once I went down there visiting afterwards – when I was about seventeen, I think. I don't think I was even shaving then – just shaving my whiskers a little bit; nothing much – just for the fun of it. Stephen was still in the Eden Hills home then.

But from there I don't know where he went after he finished school. I think he stopped around Adelaide somewhere – in the city. He joined the war when he got old enough. He went to Korea when that war started – it must have been Korea, because he had to go to Japan when the war finished.

When he came back, he came back to the army camp near Port Augusta – El Alamein. I happened to be in Port Augusta then. He still had his army clothes on and he was looking after the young recruits. I seen him then for the last time.

So I only seen him twice! He could be in Adelaide, Melbourne or Sydney driving taxis. About twelve months ago, one of the McKenzie girls saw him in Alice Springs making films. But we're like past history, me and Stephen. Yet we were close together when we were little in the Home. I believe he was the only one who cried for me when I left the Home. We're really nothing to one another now.

That's one of the effects of kids been taken away.

◆Life at Mabel Creek◆

I didn't mind leaving the Home. Work'd be some sort of a change. It was just like Syd Waye and me were sons to old Alf Turner. And David Branson, they sent him up there too.

When I got to Mabel Creek, my job was shepherding the sheep. They bought those sheep after we got there, and a few goats for their milk. That's a twelve-hour job, though. You get up at daybreak. You have to have the sheep out of the yard by sunrise. There were no paddocks in those days, no fences in the district, and we had hundreds of dingoes around.

We had to make a yard big enough for the sheep for the night and we had one there all the time – made where we stayed or where we made a camp. We made it from the dead mulga trees. We had to go and put the sheep in the yards every night. You had to make fires to keep the dingoes out. But if the fire went down, the dingoes used to know that and they used to come up. A couple of nights we heard the sheep stirring and a dingo was there. Lucky we were there sleeping in the swags. We called out and a dingo ran away.

We had to get up at daylight and by sunrise you'd be taking the sheep out of the yard to where they can have a feed and down to the big waterhole. You don't bring 'em back till sunset. We had to watch the sheep properly.

At supper time, when it was just getting sundown, we'd have meals down there at the main house. We'd have to go back soon, as the sun was going down then – back to the yards and start our fires up to keep the dingoes away. We'd be there all the rest of the night – get up at sunrise next morning (the wild dogs'd be gone away then – if there was any dingoes around). Then we'd just come back and have a feed back at the homestead and cut our lunches. We'd take out a bottle of cold tea and later, out with the sheep, make a small fire to warm the tea.

On Sundays you still have to take the sheep out. All day every day of the year. We worked for that. I had no holidays. Right through – we worked right through every year. For six or seven years we never had no spell. Me and Syd Waye, we two looked after the sheep. Yes, we were always with the sheep.

If we were camping out, especially if we were a long way out, like ten mile out at another waterhole or something with a bore, Mr Turner used to come out with us. Then he'd do what he had to do – go into the town or the station to get more food; whatever it was. We got used to it; that was our way of life, I suppose.

Syd and I had two little mobs of sheep. One mob might be wethers and weaners and rams. We'd take them to one side, and the old ewes and the lambs another side. One side, you know, keep 'em so the old sheep might just walk slowly with the little baby lambs. The other lot, the wethers and weaners and the rams'd go along a bit faster – probably further away from our camp. We'd take turns to take one mob.

And we had to still watch 'em daytime because sometimes a dingo might be round there somewhere to see the sheep walking about. It might be a dingo that wouldn't know the district and he might come in from somewhere else and he'll come across – and we'd have to just shoo him away. They'll run when they know it's a man; we're different from an animal.

We had no horses those days, so we'd have to walk – and we used to wear big hobnail boots, that's the big ones that's got some hobnails underneath so it can walk on the stony ground; a lot of stony ground around the Mabel Creek tableland there – stony place. So we used to make sure we had the good big boots when we were going around. We get used to walking; that's only simple – you've got all day. The sheep are quiet ones – they wouldn't be running; they'd just be feeding around. They was broken in – quiet; they wouldn't run away. You can just walk around them. Sheep get used to you. They're not scared of you. They know when you want to hunt 'em, move 'em along. They just walk along, whichever way you're turning them. I never had a dog.

◆ The 1939 Flood ◆

When we first started on the station at Mabel Creek, Alf Turner took some few horses from down on the farm country near Adelaide. That's when he brought a young white bloke back with him too – Don Tanner. He only brought good horses too, like a thoroughbred horse with him for his station horse. He brought up a stallion too, so he could breed some stock horses.

We were back in Mabel Creek years later, when Syd and me were still about nineteen, and one time it rained all night. We had about nine inches of rain. It started in the afternoon about four o'clock and it rained right through – just poured down like water coming out of a bucket. Must have been the biggest rain we had around that area. That filled up Lake Phillipson.

We had the sheep locked up in the yards and in the middle of the night we had to get up and open the gate and let the sheep out. The goats got washed away. Alf Turner lost those goats in 1939. It was pouring down rain. I was shepherding. The goats was left in the little creek. They didn't know; they camped in the island all right but they didn't know that island was going to get flooded. The water just came over and round and round. By the time it got high, it was too high for the goats to just walk across and the water was just too strong. It came up to their legs, knees, guts… Two goats followed the billy goat out to the channel and that saved them. The others went into the wrong creek – the main channel – and got washed away. Only about four or five made it out to the bank outside the creek. They survived, but the rest of them got hung up in the trees; the water was that strong – the 1939 Flood.

It was after that that Alf Turner was making plans to sell the sheep. There were no fences for the sheep. Now he was going to go into cattle. We took the sheep down to Lake Phillipson; we stayed there for a year to fatten them up. Lake Phillipson was part of Mabel Creek Station in those days. Dick Rankin took it after he had Mabel Creek. The Rankins kept it back on their side into Ingomar when they sold Mabel Creek.

Don Tanner was our boss, our overseer – stopping there with us in Lake Phillipson. We all knew what to do. When everything was ready, we walked the sheep to Kingoonya – around about 200 mile – then trucked them in the train to Adelaide. The boss, Alf Turner, must have went down with them from there.

Don Tanner's wife, Millie Tanner, was a Hull from Marree way – Anangu; Aboriginal woman. He was an Australian man himself – from Plympton in Adelaide. (A long time after this, I used to go down to Port Augusta all the time and visit when he was still there living with his wife.)

◆Changing Over to Cattle◆

Now Alf Turner was going to go into cattle – make Mabel Creek into a cattle station – he had to go and get some ordinary station horses, like working saddle horses for stock. So we went to Granite Downs. They called it Lambina then. One station there, named Lambina, was further down the creek from Granite Downs. The 1939 floods were everywhere. They washed away the combined homesteads and the two working girls from Oodnadatta spent the night up in the trees.

Jim Robb had good horses at Lambina. He had some breed from England and they were well bred – and that's the main one. The horse I got, it was just a skinny-looking horse.

I was thinking, 'Oh, what sort of horse am I going to get here?'

I don't know nothing about horses! So the others picked first – like Syd Waye; he seen a chestnut horse, white face and white legs. 'Oh, I'll have that one.'

Syd and a few others like David Branson took a pick what they wanted so that's the only one that was left. So I said, 'Oh, I'll take that one then.'

And the mare that I got there turned out to be a real good brood mare – you know, well bred! I found out her father came from England somewhere. I think his name was Gosford – that's what Alf Turner said Jim Robb had told him. They had only just broke in and only just kept them – Jim Robb had a lot of horses over the limit in the station at that time.

The brood mare didn't have no name – we just named it what we wanted. I named her Winsome and she was the mother of the foals I had then; she had three foals. One of the stallions came across from Anna Creek station and fathered Tommyhawk and Melody the mare, and one horse from the Twins fathered Battle Axe. Tommyhawk, Melody and

Battle Axe – one mare and two geldings. We made them into geldings. And that horse that came from Twins Station – he had well-bred blood in him as well. Glen Jacobs was at the Twins at that time – before Mr Dick Rankin bought it.

♦ They Liked Me, the Horses... ♦

When I was riding that skinny horse – the mare – when I used to ride her a bit, I was thinking, 'Oh, this horse can move a bit.' The foals grew up and I had to learn to break horses in. I just learnt by *handling* them. Oh, we watched other blokes too, but I done it in my own way. I found out to handle horses – by treating them kindly. You found that they respond to you quick that way. I used to treat 'em kindly and in no time I used to have the horses quiet.

The station manager – the boss, old Mr Turner – he needed someone to break horses in, 'cause we've got a lot of work to do. We had to have someone to break in the horses so we'll have fresh horses when they take the horses away – mustering and all that for about a month or so. They've got to have fresh horses after a month. They get tired because they're hobbled all the time; no paddocks in those days. With those two straps on their front legs, they can only just walk around a little bit. So then they have to bring 'em back and just turn them into the home paddock for a spell.

So the boss, Alf Turner, he used to come down to the yard. And this day he come down and he seen me start handling one horse and I only just broke him in not long before. He saw everybody tying their horses' legs up; tying them to the post to get the shoes off. We had to shoe the horses as that's stony country around there, Mabel Creek, so the horses won't lift anything with their foot.

This day we were going to let the horses go. They'd been working for a while and it was their turn to have a spell. Old Alf Turner came down there watching the blokes tying their horses' legs up. And he seen me get my horse and bring him up – just drop the reins on the ground and the horse waiting down there while I went and got the hammer and the chisel and the rasp to just pull the shoe off.

Then he seen me pick the horse's leg up – pick it up and just hold it while the horse was standing there. And he was thinking, 'Hey, what's this bloke! Hey! He should tie his legs up.' And he called out to me, 'Hey! He might turn and kick you!'

'No,' I said. 'He be right.'

And I just took the horse's shoe off and he just standing there with his head down and I was there holding his leg up. Old Alf Turner got the biggest shock and he gave me the job of breaking horses after that, because the other blokes' horses still wild. They can't touch a horse or the horse would kick them or something. But mine, mine were just quiet with me straightaway. That's why he gave me the job breaking in horses. Horses – I got to like horses. They liked me, the horses, straightaway.

As soon as I caught a horse, you'd see it coming up straight to me afterwards. The other horses run away when they're put in the yard. They run away from the blokes, you know. But these horses – mine – they just stand there and let me catch them, without running away.

◆The Station Hands at Mabel Creek◆

Most station hands were *A<u>n</u>angus* – Aboriginal. David Branson didn't like the station much, so Alf Turner was looking around for one bloke, Len Tuitt – a truck driver. He had his own fleet of trucks at Alice Springs or somewhere up that way. David was interested in trucks. In those days, the Alice Springs road – the Stuart Highway – used to cut right through Mabel Creek.

'Will you take him?'

'Yes,' says Len.

So David finished up in the Northern Territory somewhere. That's the last I heard of him when he left Mabel Creek.

Some station hands were whitefellas, like the overseer and the cook. Mrs Hann was cooking there for a while. She had a son, Richie, and he was the overseer – the head stockman. Mrs Turner went and left old Alf Turner – they mustn't have been getting on too well, and finish up Mr Turner married Mrs Hann.

Mary O'Toole was there then. There was a store in Coober Pedy and the storekeepers used to get their meat at Mabel Creek – when we had cattle there. We used to bring the meat – the pack bag full – into Coober Pedy here for the storekeeper. We had a little old Essex car out there. Emily Austin and Mary O'Toole probably came in on the Essex when they used to help in the store. But when it was rainy weather, then I had to come in on a pack horse; they couldn't bring the old car in – you know, you had to cut across the creeks, Long's Creek and a few other creeks. It was only a bush road and boggy. We'd come in and unload the meat and then we'd go back.

◆Stock Work, Mustering◆

'Oh,' they might say, any day when I went into Coober Pedy with the meat, 'don't come straight back when you're coming on your way home. Go round, go round the tracks.'

No paddocks, see, in those days, so in case any cattle went out on the boundary sides, we had to go around out on the north side on our way back – checking up if there were any cattle that got out.

The cattle get over the range running along. The Stuart Range runs straight from Andamooka to Mount Willoughby station to Wellbourne Hill station. One side of the land falls back this way on top of the ridge going back to Lake Phillipson – back to that country. And another part drops back to Lake Eyre country.

So we thought we'd have to go around and chase the cattle. If they go up the creek – Mabel Creek – and get too far away, they might go over the Range and go down towards Mount Barry Station – where Mount Barry now is. And we used to go out and round them up and hunt them back.

When they know it's rain, we used to go out. Then they can get water anywhere, so they probably know (animals know – instinctively) that when the land drops one way and another, they know there'll be a big creek somewhere. So they go – they follow a little small creek down and they know it's getting bigger and bigger and by the time they get down a bit further, there're gum trees and water holes. That's why we just pull 'em back before they go out – before they go outside Mabel Creek.

When they're going to have a muster – say at that place that was called Nilpinna in those days – they'd ring up the other station blokes and they'd tell them, 'Oh, we're having a muster coming around very soon. So you better come and check up and see if any of your cattle there.' They might ring up Oodnadatta way or Anna Creek.

So we used to go and see. We'd all come there from different places and we'd go out mustering all the cattle that's there at Nilpinna. See, at Nilpinna, they might want to truck some cattle away – their own cattle. So we all come – and Anna Creek might be the first one to go – want to go back. He might want to go back next day. So they muster the cattle up and he'll cut his bullocks out first if there's any. Every man got their own horses that cuts out their bullocks. Whoever's in charge, cuts out their bullocks. And his stockmen would take the cattle back to Anna Creek.

There were no paddocks. They know the boss'll call out for the muster. Or even they might sing out for the muster – at Anna Creek. 'Oh, we'll come up when you have a muster.'

In those days, they had what the Flying Doctors use – they had Flynn's two-way radio. All the stations had those. You could talk to one another. You might make a time when you're going to talk to one another. And if somebody didn't come to the muster – they might be behind – they'd sing out to them on the two-way radio, 'Oh, we found some of your bullocks!' Just to let them know.

And that station might only send a couple of blokes down then to get those bullocks. Musterers'd just put them to one side and the other station blokes'd take 'em back then.

◆ The Americans ◆

That was the time when those army blokes were going up to Alice Springs – Americans. In those days, the highway went through Mabel Creek. They see nobody on the roads. They see one bloke – me. They couldn't make it out that I was there sitting on my own looking after the bullocks. I was pumping water for the horses and cattle that camped there. I was making sure the tanks keep full in the wind. It drops, see. On a windy day the pump – the windmill – would have been filling the tank. But on a calm day you use the engine to pump the water into the tank.

These were the first two Yankees I ever seen in my whole life. I couldn't believe how they talked.

'What are you doing out here on your *own*? Aren't you scared out here on your own?'

It was just before the big rain came. I wasn't frightened. I was on my own; I lost my mother and father. You grow up real quick on your own. You just got yourself. You don't worry.

I couldn't make it out how they talked – that words come out so musical. A lot came up to Coober Pedy once, oh a long time after that. They were on holidays. They paid Bob McKenzie for one day bulldozing. I was checking behind for them – this side of the airstrip. The woman's voice was so musical. I didn't know English would be so musical. Australians talk plain.

While I was at Mabel Creek, we went to Tieyon Station. The boss, old Alf Turner, had to get some wagon horses from old Frank Smith. Tieyon Station is just on the boundary of South Australia and Northern Territory – straight level east of Kulgera, just going towards Finke Station.

That's where I got my next horse. Old Frank, he had too many horses at his station. He gave old Alf some horses there so they could break them in for saddle horses but mainly he went to get the wagon horses.

The old bloke asked me did I want a horse.

'Yes, I'll take a horse.'

'I've got too many horses,' he said. 'You can have that one if you want it.'

And he give me one little black mare, a little young one – so I took it. 'Yeah, all right.'

So I come away with one horse. I already had Battle Axe, the mother back at Mabel Creek. We used to call this little mare *Kuyai* because she was black. They used to call little girls *Kuyai*. (And the boys were called *Wiyai*.)

◆Leaving Mabel Creek◆

I was at Mabel Creek for ten years and they treated me and Syd just like sons. We were allowed to go in the house and we used to have a feed in their house. But the other blokes out in the camps, they were one side. They had their meals in the sand or out on the woodheap in those days. I wasn't in a camp before. I was straight out of a Home, so they treated me like a son. No money, though, that's the only trouble. Good old man, though, but that's what it was like in those days. Nothing! I was working for nothing! I got about twenty-eight pound all the time I was at Mabel Creek.

But I decided if I'm not getting any pay I'll make sure I take my horses with me – I've got *something* to show for working. I broke the little horse in as I was leaving Mabel Creek – that was Battle Axe. The old mother died a long time ago. At the time I took off, Tommyhawk was just a young colt, a young horse just broken in. (But he was big enough and old enough to travel down there to the Kingoonya Races like he did.)

At the time, I broke in too. She was a stock horse, not really a racer but a good thoroughbred – like a sire. I kept her as a breeder at Mabel Creek and just let her go out into the paddock with the other horses and she had two foals and I took them when I went to Ingomar. Old Jack Giles had given me one horse from Wellbourne Hill – a good solid horse. He turned out a good cattle horse, a good working horse, so I made him into a pack horse just to go from Mabel Creek to Ingomar… But I was supposed to be going through – travel right through to Queensland. I'd made up my mind to go on the drovings with the horses I had. I was going to go to Marree and catch the drover. The drover used to bring all the cattle into Marree and truck the cattle there on the railway line. And I was going to catch one of those teams, because they needed blokes all the time, especially a bloke with horses.

I had to go right out to a place called Camel Flat twenty or thirty mile out from Mabel Creek – to get the horse. I had to get up early one morning and look for him and find him and bring him back.

Old Alf Turner, he tried to stop me and said, 'Oh, you can't go now!'

But I said, 'No, I'm going. I've made up my mind. I'm going. I'm going to Queensland. I've done all my work for you here.' I had a mind of my own too. 'I got my own horses – I got nothing else, so I'm getting out while I can.'

I put a pack saddle on my horse – old Alf Turner gave me one pack saddle that he had. I put all my gear and that, my swag, tucker, water can.

When I was going out, going through, I ran into Ian – Ian Rankin. He was a young bloke then. He used to come to Mabel Creek and worked there. He must have gone home and told his father I was going to go through. Yeah, when I was travelling through with my horses I asked the Rankins if I might stop a day.

'OK. You can stop as long as you like. You can even work here if you want to,' the father said.

◆Life at Ingomar◆

I found out I was going to get good pay there – five pound a week. More than I was getting at Mabel Creek all the time I was there.

See, they knew I was an experienced worker. They used to just tell me to go. 'Oh, you can just go anywhere, mustering.' They wouldn't tell me what to do. They'd say, 'We're mustering that paddock this morning. Oh, you can go out.'

I could just go where I think the sheep are and bring 'em in without them telling me where. They can't tell you, 'You go out this road and that road to get the sheep and bring them.' I'd just go! I'd know where to go.

I used my own horse because my horse was experienced. I'd just go behind some of the sheep, sometimes with some of my horses. There's paddocks down Ingomar country. They'd just have sheep running along the fence and I'd take them home towards the station. I'd just throw the saddle reins over the horse's neck and he'd walk along behind me. I'd be walking along a bit further over and he's hunting the sheep along – like another man helping along. I wouldn't have to ride him – he'd walk along behind the sheep. Yes, he was a good horse. I never had a dog, but the horses, they'd do anything.

Marty's brother Stephen Dodd as a baby, c. 1928: 'That was how he came down from Oodnadatta.' The first Colebrook Home at Quorn (established 1927) can be seen in the background. (Photo courtesy of the State Library of South Australia and Faith Thomas.)

Second Colebrook Home, Quorn, c. 1932. Marty Dodd is at far right, second back row. (Photo courtesy of the State Library of South Australia and Faith Thomas.)

Chopping wood, Colebrook House, Quorn, c. 1934.
'I used to be the one that's cutting the wood for the kitchen.'
L to R: Stephen Dodd, Steven O'Donoghue, Marty Dodd.
(Photo courtesy of the State Library of South Australia and Faith Thomas.)

Children gathering firewood, Colebrook Home, Quorn, 1934. 'And Saturdays, that'd be six armfuls.
This must have been a Saturday – other kids helping.'
L to R: Ruby Hayes (Freddy Hayes behind), Willy Taylor/Steven O'Donoghue (head turned),
Eileen O'Donoghue, Faith Coulthard, George Tongerie, David Branson, Ray Lester, Marty Dodd.
(Photo courtesy of the State Library of South Australia and Faith Thomas.)

Boys in Colebrook Home uniform, 1939. Stephen Dodd fourth from left, then George Tongerie.
(Photo courtesy of the State Library of South Australia and Faith Thomas.)

Marty Dodd and Stephen Dodd, c. 1938.
'I came down from Mabel Creek Station to visit my little brother Stephen at Colebrook Home. I was a working bloke by then.'
(Photo courtesy of the State Library of South Australia and Faith Thomas.)

Marty Dodd, Archie Lang – 'my best mate' – and Henry Brown helping to build Ingomar Station house. Clem Fitzgerald was the builder. (Photo courtesy of the Rankin family.)

*Marty Dodd with Windy in the iron stockyard, Ingomar Station.
'Windy was just a working horse, but fast over short distances. He won about ten stockhorse races at
Kingoonya, Oodnadatta and Tarcoola. Ian Rankin used to ride him.'
(Photo courtesy of Marie Nourse [née O'Leary].)*

Clem Fitzgerald's children at Ingomar Station. Ian Fitzgerald is on the right. (Photo courtesy of Marie Nourse [née O'Leary].)

Fencing, Ingomar Station. The yards can be seen in the background.

'The Father', Tommy Dodd (Tjundaga), 1940.
(Photo courtesy of State Library of SA, Mountford Sheard Collection/Ara Irititja Archive.)

Tommy Dodd receiving the Queen's Medal (British Empire Medal) at Amata, 1971. (Photo courtesy of Bill Edwards.)

Tommy Dodd dressed for church held outside his house at Amata. (Photo courtesy of State Library of SA, David Hewitt Collection/Ara Irititja Archive.)

◆Battle Axe at the Kingoonya Races◆

All the time we'd be taking the horses down to Kingoonya. Finish up, my good horse, the little one I used to call Battle Axe – he finished up winning three Cups there at Kingoonya; two Kingoonya Cups and another race. We had a race meeting in October – just a gymkhana. The Kingoonya Cup used to be Easter time.

My old friend, Clem Fitzgerald, he lived at Bulgunnia Station, that's sixty mile out of Tarcoola and sixty mile from Ingomar, about halfway in-between. (Ian Fitzgerald, a taxi bloke in Port Augusta now – that's his son. He comes up here a lot of times, bringing people up here to Coober Pedy. I've known him from when he was a little kid when his father came working at Ingomar.)

Anyway, Clem Fitzgerald, he seen that young horse Battle Axe when I was going to Tarcoola, through Bulgunnia. He said, 'I want a horse. I want a horse for Kingoonya Races.' He was talking about it, about the gymkhana meeting, and then he said, 'Oh, what about that young horse there?'

'Yeah, you can have him. You can use him.'

He fed him with chaff like you train a racehorse; hand fed him in the paddock. Just keep him in the yard, training him there. He didn't know nothing about riding a horse but he had a good horse to look after. Yes, I let him have Battle Axe for that race. But they had no horse rider, so they asked a bloke that knew; one of the Mabel Creek workers, Don Tanner. He's a white man but he was working at Mabel Creek for a long time – he's my friend for years and years. So we got him to ride the horse. We had no other – you see, a black boy couldn't ride it. If they could, I could have ridden it myself – but I would have put a lighter weight than me – something about ten stone or less. I've never been under eleven stone – spread over because I'm a bit tall. Not that heavy for a horse, I suppose, 'cause they use to carry me quite easily when I train 'em. They're strong horses. Then, in the race, when they feel a man on them two stone lighter or something like that, makes quite a difference in the weight on the back.

Well, on that day, they raced him, tried him out at Kingoonya. When the race started, you know – the horses are ready. I used to learn him to jump off the mark. When you train a horse, you've got to let the horse's head go straightaway. Well, he was used to that and he felt this bloke touch him on the ribs. He was *gone*, flat out like a shot! In the first race he went in, that bloke was hanging on. He thought the horse was bolting! He pulled him all the way – he didn't let him go. I don't know how many lengths he would have won by – that was only a six-furlong race.

I was thinking, 'Oh, he's lucky he won that race!'

That bloke, Don Tanner, he was still holding him when he rode round the corner. He couldn't pull up at the winning post, he just kept going – he couldn't pull up. Finished up he was standing up in the stirrups! He didn't know how to ride it. He was *scared* of the horse! It galloped. You know, when a horse goes that fast, he thought the horse was bolting and he was hanging on to his head. But the horse always puts his head lower down when he gallops, for the air to go right through his throat, I suppose, where it's got more room. Old Don didn't know about riding him – just hanging on – but he won the race. Not that *he* won it – the horse won it!

That was an ordinary race. It must have been the October Meeting, 'cause Clem Fitzgerald was feeding him with chaff. Clem lived at Ingomar with his family. Clem knew me from a young kid. He was a bulldozer driver and a dam maker. I took the horse back home after we had finished racing it, happy about him winning.

◆ The Kingoonya Cup... ◆

Colin Hayes (later on, he ended up training some Melbourne Cup winners, himself) came up to visit Mr Rankin a few times. We was training horses for the Kingoonya Races and Colin Hayes just looked at them. He knows what horse is going to win the race. He didn't say nothing but he could tell by the look of it which horse was fit – the condition of the horse. I used to get up at four o'clock or five o'clock to train 'em while the air is cool.

We had to travel in for the Kingoonya Cup. From Ingomar, everyone would go to the Kingoonya Cup. We had to take Battle Axe in and put him in the paddock. It was a grass meeting – a grass-fed meeting – so the horses can be all equal when they start in the race and we all had to take them in the month before so no one can cheat. The Kingoonya Racing Committee would weigh them later for correct weight.

This time it was the Cup Race. Battle Axe was against The Monk; it came in from Mr Billy Robbins at Tarcoola. The Monk should have been good enough to beat all the horses there. But Battle Axe, he was what they call a front runner; takes off and leaves the galloping horses behind. Ian Rankin was a fairly good jockey and he knew how to ride Battle Axe. He don't hold his mouth – just let his head go; just lets him gallop freely. They just couldn't catch him – he'd just keep going! The Monk was trying to catch up but got too far behind. Came second. And he'd run third in the Melbourne Cup!

◆...and the Oodnadatta Cup◆

They used to have a race at Oodnadatta every year in May, so I decided to ask Mr Rankin if I could take the horse up there for the races – usually they let me take it for the holiday.

He said, 'Yes, you can have your holiday then. You can take it.'

So I took off from Ingomar, went around through to Mount Penrhyn, come up here to Mabel Creek, and out from Mabel Creek I used to go straight across to Oodnadatta, cut across country – there was no roads going there from Mabel Creek so I had to head straight for a place called Mount Barry. (Now the road's there, all right, going right through these days.) But – I got caught in the rain, heavy rain – just over the Breakaways just there, where the main highway goes – now it's the Breakaway country on that side.

I was stuck there about three or four days and the creek was running flooded, and Mr Rankin was ringing up from Ingomar, ringing up to mob camp and saying, 'Oh, you seen Marty coming up there yet?'

'No, he never turned up.'

They know the creek's all flooded. Bob Kemp, the boss of Mount Barry Station, was asking, 'Oh, perhaps he cut across to the river, the creek or something?'

Glen Rankin said, 'No, he wouldn't do that, he would stop, so he must be camping somewhere.'

Sure enough, about five days after, I turned up there to Mount Barry. They stopped ringing one another then after Bob Kemp told my boss, 'Oh, he's turned up here, and he's not going to stop tonight, he's got to keep going, he's going to keep going towards Oodnadatta – because there's another rain coming up. Clouds been making up – all heavy ones. Rained all night.'

So I'd said to him, 'I'd better go, I think, Bob.'

He said, 'Yeah, righto.'

When I got to Oodnadatta, another rain caught me there. They had a big meeting, and after it they said, 'Race has got to be postponed for six weeks.'

Yes, six weeks in Oodnadatta – sitting out in the sandhills! I had enough money – I'd saved up enough money, just to buy flour and things like that – tinned meat mostly from the Oodnadatta store. I was right there – and Mr Rankin rang up and said, 'You can please yourself what you do – either go or you stop there.'

'No,' I said. 'I'll wait and sit down here.'

I'd travelled them horses all up on foot, two of mine and a couple of Ian Rankin's. I took them all up on foot, they just travelled – well, you can only travel about twenty miles a day with the horse when you're walking them. Yes, twenty miles a day, that's a fair way, thirty kilometres. Every day we'd go about that far and I used to worry about how I'm going to get on at night time with these horses out in brumby country – a lot of brumby horses in that country at that time. I was thinking, 'They might get mixed up with the brumbies and gallop away.' But it finished up good. These horses used to only go a little way, about half a mile, then they turn round and come back towards me at night time and camp close to me.

'Oh, that's good,' I used to think. 'These horses, look, they're camping near me.' Most other people's horses, they go a long way – they don't stop with their owners and bosses, they run away. They might be chasing them for about five or six miles next morning, but these horses, when I went to the sand hills, they just stopped not far from me; they never went away in Oodnadatta.

We had a Cup horse – that was Battle Axe. The blokes that like to take the weights, the stewards was all there in the yards, taking the names of the horses. Showed my two horses there and Ian had sent a couple of his horses up with me for the race too.

But the bloke from the Finke thought his horse was going to win the Oodnadatta Cup. The jockey and the owner were looking and Ian

Rankin asked them, when all the horses are standing around, 'What do you reckon? See, he's in the yard – our Cup horse. Which one do you reckon is the Cup horse out of those horses?'

They looking around and they picked a big tall horse. Tommyhawk was standing there – the brother of the horse.

'Oh, wrong. You're wrong. See that little short horse standing over there, he's our Cup horse.'

Oh, you ought to have seen them blokes. They laughed. Yeah, when they looked at the little short horse alongside their horse, he's about two hands higher. Oh, they laughed when they see this horse.

'Oh, gee, we've got the Cup won,' they reckon. 'Oh, we'll have two Kingoonya Cups, and one Oodnadatta Cup now,' they thinking.

So Ian got to ride that day. He's a very good rider, Ian Rankin. He didn't ask me what do you got to do. He just knew he had to let the horse go. Didn't matter about how far he had to go. He'd still stay in the front. They had two horses in that race, the Finke mob, because they reckon they'll run that other horse fast, keep him, knock him up when he goes about halfway. My horse'll be knocked up by the time he has to gallop with this other horse, they're thinking. That's their strategy.

But no – Battle Axe ran. The big horse supposed to gallop along from behind. But they didn't know any little short horse could run so fast from the beginning. He took off from the beginning, he's five lengths in the front as soon as he took off.

'Oh, we'll catch him in a minute,' that bloke riding the first horse reckoned.

The start was way over the far side, They had to go around about one and a half times. They had to go right around, then come back. Oodnadatta course is a long way round.

So when they were going along, when they took off up here and Battle Axe took off in the lead, 'Oh, we'll catch him in a minute,' they thought.

But he was still five lengths in the front when he went past the first time. Ian just let him have his head. When he got halfway round, they're getting a bit closer. They got a bit close but he had 'em stretched out by that time – like Brown's cows, as they say, you know, coming behind one another. By the time they got around, back to the starting post, he was still five lengths in front, ten metres in front. And when he come around there, Ian let him have his head a bit. And he was just coming down there on his own. Down to the winning post, down the straight. Ian's smiling, a big smile on his face, old Ian Rankin.

And the people on the stands, they were stunned. They never seen a horse run like that, over a mile and half, take the lead and just go all the way. Keep further and further. When he got down there, he was about ten or twelve lengths in the front, coming down the straight. And that other racehorse, theirs the Finke Cup horse, they were blown, they'd really had it. They'd had it by the time they come round there. They were just cantering behind, couldn't keep up. They don't know how.

That bloke come to me after and said, 'Oh jings, you know that horse of yours, he can win the Alice Springs Cup, no worries at all.' He'd been to the Alice racing a lot of times. He seen no one race like that. He told me straight out that horse could win the Alice Springs Cup. That's a mile and a half.

They couldn't believe it. They were stunned watching the race – there was no singing out at all. They all lost their money too. Yeah, they lost their money on their horse.

Only one bloke was glad, that bloke from Anna Creek. His name was Archie McLean, he used to be on the station there, he was ready to father that horse. He was going to take Battle Axe across to Anna Creek for a while. He was so glad, he turned around and give me twenty pounds. He said, 'Oh that's for training the horse like that. That was great.'

After the race, I didn't go up to get the Cup, even though Battle Axe was my horse. Everyone knew that I was the trainer. And after that race, there was no more one and a half mile races. He'd won the mile and a half race in Oodnadatta. He won it that easily and by that far that they wouldn't have a race like that again.

But we took him up there again, but it was only a mile race. That was nothing for him; he won that Cup a second time. We thought about going to Alice Springs. We'd go there early enough, you only go twenty-five miles a day, that's ordinary walking pace for a horse. That's exercise too. That's like training them – you don't have to gallop them, they get their wind from walking, long walks. Trotting just along, they exercise themselves all the time, their muscles are loose, they get a lot of strength in their legs. Going on a long trip like that I'd have my own horse, my riding horse. But I might ride Battle Axe once, just to give him a bit of practice, but I wouldn't ride him any more. He's already fit. So if you'd walk him that far, you just train him a little bit by cantering around in the sand hills when it's getting a bit closer to the race.

But I decided I wouldn't go to Alice Springs. Rosie my daughter was sick with double pneumonia. I know he was good enough anyway for what he'd done. He won about five Cups altogether – all around Kingoonya. They brought a horse from Adelaide to try and beat him there. They couldn't beat him. Not really, no, not in a race. Only one, one useless bloke ride him once there, he didn't know how to ride him and he pulled him up, never gave him a chance.

I never really rode him in a race – I was too heavy – but I trained him. Oh, they know, they know – I'd put on him a bloke that knows him – well he'd just let him have his head. He'd get so many lengths in front and he won't let them horses get any closer. If there's one horse getting closer, he'd just put his pace on, a little bit faster. He wasn't a very big horse, but I don't know how he was that easy a galloper. He'd gallop so easily!

See, Battle Axe's father run third in the Sydney Cup, and that's a two-mile race, so he's got good breeding on the mother's side, so that's good blood from England – English horse and from Sydney, New South Wales. They brought that stallion back to the Twins. McTaggert from the Twins gave it to Mr Rankin, to keep it there, at Mabel Creek. So he had good blood, breeding in him.

◆Mustering the Sheep◆

I might have been just getting near twenty when I left Mabel Creek and then I stayed on Ingomar anywhere between ten to fifteen years, I suppose. A long time I was there. When the other blokes come in from Port Augusta or Port Pirie in busy times, they get the same pay – five pound a week in the busy season.

I was one of the main musterers. They send me out on the paddock to get all the sheep in. They might say, 'Bring in four hundred' or 'Today we'll need six hundred.' They'll count the night before and let me know. See, they knew I was an experienced worker with bullocks. They used to tell me just to go – 'Oh, you can just go anywhere mustering.' I'd know where to go. I might go to the paddock where the sheep are and I'll cut off so many. I'd just count – give it a rough count. 'Oh that might be four hundred,' I'd think, and cut 'em off and bring 'em back. A little over four hundred I'd get, to make sure that I'd be not too short. Shearers wouldn't want to be stopped working. They'd want to be keeping going. Or I might only cut out about three hundred, something like that, and then get another three hundred – guess that second lot and that'd be six hundred. I wouldn't count the lot.

And you can't bring in fresh sheep – they're too heavy. You have to stop them overnight in the yard. Otherwise, the dew gets on them or they're too full from water and food, from eating overnight. So they sit down – they camp in the yards overnight – no feed – and they're nice and light then for the shearers. I'd just grab them and pull them out easy from the pens. Generally they're heavy – their stomachs real round and full – but their stomachs have gone down flat by the time they stop in the yard – twelve hours. When they get shorn, they get let out straight to the paddock then and that's when they can have a feed.

◆The Changeover to Motorbikes◆

When I first worked, I was riding horses before the motorbikes and Toyotas came in. When the mustering changed, when they had Toyotas and motorbikes, it wouldn't take long to go out to the paddock and get the sheep. It changed the way of working a bit – we used to just sit on the motorbikes.

You never gallop a horse – you just let 'em walk, because they'll have a busy day working, bringing in the sheep. But a motorbike can go flat out, get out there and bring 'em in. You could be half bringing them in with a motorbike by the time you got out there with a horse. The motorbike just goes right around, and all the sheep run in because they hear the motorbike coming and they get together. With a horse they don't know you're coming and you've just got to go around and get 'em in a little mob so that they're in. A horse is a lot slower.

The changeover didn't surprise me – you could see it coming. You know, it's a lot easier. I rode the motorbike for about ten or fifteen years.

And when we changed over to motorbikes, the horses didn't mind. They just let the horses out in the paddock for a spell – they were happy then, too, the horses. They used to come every weekend to check out to see me. It's funny, you know, there's a little paddock around the house out at Ingomar and horses used to go around that paddock to the big paddock and on Saturday – they seemed to know when it was the weekend – I don't know how they know – they used to come and wait around near the corner and I'd wait around and open the gate and let them in. They'd just walk into the water and have a drink – a trough and all was there. I used to brush them down. They liked to come down to see me.

I had some kids too – station kids – they used to come down in the yard, rush down there. They used to jump on the horses, ride 'em round in the yard. One girl works here now in Coober Pedy. Marie O'Leary her name was (I don't know what her married name is). She was only a little girl, five or six when she first seen me. And she was getting a bit bigger when I took off from Ingomar. That little girl used to ride Powder Puff. We called her that because she had a little white patch on her nose. The other little foal was called Windy – born on a windy night in September. He won about ten races later on, and he won the first race he started in – a four-furlong race.

◆ The Main Musterer ◆

Yes, before I go mustering, the boss'd tell me maybe after supper, might be in the afternoon, that I'd have to go and get some sheep in the morning. And if they were a fair way or a long way out, I'd just get up, say about half past six, as soon as it would get light, and before sunrise. I'd go out and muster the sheep with a motorbike and bring 'em in close and then come home for breakfast – that'd be about half past seven or eight o'clock. The sheep'd be walking towards the wool shed paddock and I'd just go out after breakfast and bring 'em in.

Usually I was the main musterer for that part of it. I'd do that – go out early and get them. The others might come out when I'm nearly finished, got 'em all rounded up; they might come out and start bringing the sheep in then and I'd go and have breakfast.

Oh, if you know what you're doing, one person can do it. But that's the trouble, not too many blokes know what to do. They can't understand the way the animal thinks and they don't know where they'd be. But I'd have an idea. I'd just go straight out to where I think they'd be and just usually run into them all right. And I turn them back then, in the scrub paddock.

My word, you had to know what you were doing. When you've lived amongst animals, you know what area they're going to go. Now for instance, on a windy day, you just check out what way the wind's blowing from – it might be blowing from the west – well, you know the sheep're out that side; sheep go towards wind or any animals go because they can smell the food, the grass and that, growing in that direction. They just walk straight towards it. 'That wind's been blowing for about twelve hours now,' I might be thinking – and you know that's the west side of the paddock, so you say, 'I'll go round to get them at that other bend and they'll be probably on that fence and turn 'em all in from that side.'

One little bloke came up from Adelaide, one white bloke, following me flat out on his motorbike saying, 'I wonder where this bloke's going – we can't see any sheep in this paddock.' Next minute there's a big lot of sheep out in the paddock. 'Hey! How do you do this?' He couldn't work out how we got the sheep because 'We're lost in the paddock,' he was thinking. 'Must have been lost.' He was just following me along.

A lot of stockmen are like that and they know where the sheep are.

The earlier you go out, the closer the sheep they'll be together. But later in the day they spread out a bit, you know. The slower ones mightn't be walking very fast. The fast ones'll go faster and they'll get spread out. But in the night they usually get together. I think they get together about midnight. They know where other sheep are and they just camp there all together and, as soon as it gets daybreak, they spread out then and they're gone.

But you might go out early and just catch 'em, when they're just spreading out – round 'em up before they split up too much. You just cut up the ones you reckon you'd need. See, he might have told me, 'Oh yeah, you might bring in a thousand.' I might bring in a thousand that day.

That other left from whatever I bring in, we just turn 'em out into the night paddock. That's at the end of that station paddock near the woolshed. From there, all I've got to do Friday morning is just get out around there and muster them in – in the close home paddock. There's a lot of feed in that home paddock. It's kept specially for shearing times.

But if it looked like rain, they'd get them in a little bit earlier before the rain. They might lock 'em up so that they make sure they'll get enough dry ones. If they're all wet, shearers would just have a day off.

There might be six or seven or might be eight shearers on that board, you know. So they grab the sheep going out pretty quick when they're shearing. They're two hundred a day men, you know – more than that. Shearers – they go fast like that. Say, there's three or four blokes like that, that can get up to two hundred sheep, there's a lot of sheep going through. See, there's four lots of work; one lot before smoko, another lot before dinner, that's every two hours, and there's one after dinner and one before knock-off time to quarters.

The sheep are all inside the Dog Fence which is just inside of Ingomar. When you come out from Brumby Creek, there's one yard with a high fence. That's where the sheep are – inside that paddock. Since they got that in this last thirty years, they made another paddock – outside the netting: the Dog Fence. That paddock fence comes right around outside, from down that way, comes out around the netting then it goes out to that side of Mabel Creek, and that's dingo-proof. They have to keep fixing the fence because going up and down sometimes it might rain, the creek might flood, there might be water to knock it down or a kangaroo might make a hole in it.

They mainly had sheep at Ingomar in those days but they had the bullocks out at the outside paddock. And, in the meantime, I think the Rankins got Mount Penrhyn station. That's the paddock on this side of Ingomar – they used to turn the cattle out there.

◆ Finding the Father Again ◆

When I had the new green Chev, I went down to Port Augusta to pick up my brother Andy and brought him up to Mimili to see our father. It was about the same time as when the photo of me was taken at Ingomar building the station homestead – about 1951 or '52. That was the first time I seen my father since I went into the Home. I was about thirty then. Sammy was only sixteen.

Later again, when I went to see him at Amata when I was about fifty, when I went to see him in my Chev truck, I turned and ask my father, 'When I was in the Home, why didn't you come and visit me?'

He told me, 'I don't know. I didn't think you'd like – like to see me visit you.'

I said, 'Of course I would'a. You was my father!'

You can't change anything else, you know. Once you've got your mother and father, you can't change that. He thought I mightn't want to visit him. I was only working in Mabel Creek – he could have easy come down there to see me once.

'I didn't know where you was,' he said, 'till years after.'

When I first went to Mabel Creek, years before, somebody told me that he was living at Wellbourne Hill at the time. Wellbourne Hill was not far from Marla Bore, the first station nearest to Marla Bore going eastwards on the Oodnadatta road. Once, we went from Mabel Creek to get the horses at Tieyon Station. We went through to Wellbourne Hill and seen one of the stockman and he told me that my Dad was there somewhere. But I was the bloke looking after the horses, so I had to keep going. And then the time we were on our way back, he'd gone to Wallatinna Station. I think he was building yards up around there for the station people – Granite Downs had Wallatinna too. It was still Jim Robb's.

Yes, I asked him straight out, 'Why didn't you visit me so I could find out?'

And he thought different way: 'Oh, he mightn't like to see me.'

But I told him, 'I'm your son. You could easily visit me!'

That can't change anything. He must have thought it was all right when I talk like that to him. And he come and stayed with me for a little while then. I took him back after he had a holiday here and not long after that he passed away. I went and stopped with him in Amata for a while, you know, when I took him back. That's where he stayed when he was getting old. He had his little pension house there at Amata – under one of them big trees.

◆The Father Passes Away◆

And when he passed away, I didn't know nothing about it. Sadie Singer from Indulkana – that's my cousin (she calls me brother all the time, through the mother and the father) – she told me. She said, 'Oh, I heard through the grapevine that your father passed away.'

I was working at Mabel Creek again. After I been travelling round here and there, working for Mr Rankin, I went back to Mabel Creek.

And Mr Brown was here then in Coober Pedy, Neita Brown's husband. So I went and seen him. I said, 'Oh, is that true that my father passed away?'

He rung up Amata and find out. 'Oh, did Tommy Dodd pass away up there?'

They said, 'Yes' from up there. They said a couple of blokes from here in Coober Pedy, they jumped on a plane and went up – some of the Government blokes. When they heard the news they went and visit him, you know, to be at the funeral.

He blew them all up. He said, 'Hey! You should have got in touch – you knew he had a son, Martin Dodd. You should have rung him up so he could get up there to the funeral.'

Didn't bother to ring up. I was just finished working in Mabel Creek at the time. When I'd come back, I had three hundred pounds in cash too. I could have got a ride there straightaway I found out.

And I asked them, 'Did Sammy go to the funeral?'

And they said, 'No. He didn't go.'

That's my younger brother that stopped with him all the time. When we went into the Home, he was born after that – about twenty or thirty years after that, from another mother – from my mother's sister. He turned around and married my mother's sister. (See, you might marry one girl and she's got sisters and she might die young and the sister is the nearest one that you can marry straightaway if you want to. That's good – that's their law again. It's not wrong; it's the right thing. And a woman is happier to have the sister's husband than somebody else.)

I think Sammy was back at Mimili. I think he knew but he mightn't have thought to go to the funeral. Caught in his own way – his own little business – whatever he's doing. He must respect, but he just didn't think. Or he could have had a broken-down car that day; I don't know what happened. But made me feel worse when I heard he didn't go either. And he – the father – got buried there at that time.

◆ The Medal from the Queen ◆

A few years before that, the Government bloke went up there. I think it was the South Australian Chief of Police – he went up there to give him a medal from the Queen. I had that medal and I gave it to Sammy. I said, 'Oh, you look after the medal because I travel around too much.'

And he turned around and give it to somebody. I'm not sure who he is but he's at Amata. He give him the medal.

I said, 'Oh, you shouldn't have done that. You shouldn't have given that medal. If I had've known you were going to give that medal, I would have got it.' But I was travelling around too much. And I was thinking, 'Oh, he might keep the medal. He's settled down in one place all the time.' He was closer to his father because his father grew him up. He never grew us up. He wanted us.

In those days, no people was drinking. They were on the Reserve or in the station country. The parents and even the relations love you just the same – they love you. Doesn't matter who the father is – we're still the mother's child; they still want you.

Yes, Sammy was supposed to have been closer to his father, him, my brother. But he never respected that, never kept it. He was brought up in the bush camps. He didn't think the medal worth keeping. But he should have kept it with pride and joy, to share, a precious thing like that, with the grandchildren and great-grandchildren. I respected Father all the time. But he doesn't – he didn't respect. Might have been his attitude.

Yes, they went up there to give him the medal and I've got the photo of him getting the medal from the Commissioner of the Police.

See, in that Ooldea country – Nullarbor Plain – he'd been in that area. The Old People, they'd showed him all that land where all the blowholes and all the caves. And he showed it to the Government people where all those caves are. All over in the Nullarbor Plains. He knew where all that was. Yes, the Old People, some of the ones that went to Ooldea, they showed him. He was well known to everybody.

◆ Married Life ◆

They have a men's hut at Ingomar, alongside the station homestead, it might be just about fifty yards from the main homestead, and they just ring the bell in the morning and you'd go and have breakfast then – probably at the kitchen table. Yes, I used to have my meals in the kitchen; me and whoever else was working there. Sometimes Henry Brown, sometimes Billy Brown, Darby Gilbert and Archie Lang.

Archie, my little mate, was only a little small kid running around at Mabel Creek but, when he got down to Ingomar, he was a working boy then. So he used to come in handy for helping. When I first got to Ingomar, the station family were living in a tumbledown sort of shack. They built the good house then – that's the photo of me and Archie Lang and Henry Brown helping Clem Fitzgerald build that house.

After a few years, Jack Lang and his wife was living there at Ingomar and there was a girl come along – their daughter named Rita. So I got to know her. The old bloke, her father, came down from Coober Pedy here and he had the job of helping in the shearing yards. He'd do that at shearing time or crutching time. He used to yard the sheep into the pens for the shearers.

Rita came from Umeewarra Mission in Port Augusta. She went down there as a schoolgirl with her big sister, Lena. Lena went later on up to Darwin way – she's still up there.

And after a while I had my first little son – Johnny. He was born at Tarcoola – that's the nearest hospital. I was over there at Ingomar Station and it was just close; saved them sending Rita down to Port Augusta. The Rankins arranged for that. And I had a car then and so I drove the car down – a little truck.

Yes, my wife's father's family when they came in from Coober Pedy camped out by the woolshed. That's not far from the station, about a quarter mile. They'd camp out there in the camp. They'd make their own wurley or *ka*<u>*n*</u>*ku*.

She was with me for the while. We had another little hut there. I used to live in the hut. She grew up down at Umeewarra and came back to Ingomar after schooling – back to her mother and father. She went down when she was just starting to get to school age, so she was quite accustomed to living in the camp, she didn't worry. She was a fairly quiet sort of a person. I was a bit older.

We had four sons and three daughters. They were born in different places. The one son was born there, Tarcoola. Then after that, that hospital was pulled down; the Sisters finished that hospital. So the other kids were born down Port Augusta way. I had the car so I took her almost every time. I just used to wait around until the time was up for the baby to be born – and come back with them. I had my swag. I'd just stop anywhere; I was used to lying out in the open – in the country.

It was different when I was married; we would get a lot more stores then and she'll cook the feeds for me and the kids. My wife was a good cook. I think she'd learnt most of it in the Home. So the kids'd have a good feed all the time when they was little.

Yes, I'd got married – we went to Port Augusta to get married in the Methodist Church. I had a little Chev truck, by that time. We came straight back to Ingomar to work.

I worked all the time. I was one of the main station hands at Ingomar. From when I was about twenty I worked there. I was going away for a while to Mabel Creek, then I went back to Ingomar. There were the same bosses there later on. The Rankins had bought Mabel Creek by then.

Towards the end of my station life at Ingomar I did all the stock work. They had three stations – Twins, McDouall Peake and Ingomar. There were usually a couple of blokes there working – when they need it. But see, when they really need 'em, they just send to Port Augusta or somewhere and pick the boys up that know all about stock – to bring 'em there for the shearing or crutching; *A*<u>*n*</u>*angu* – Aboriginal stockmen. Raymond Wingfield was one of them.

◆Over on the West Coast◆

I left the horses there when I took off to move into Coober Pedy. Left them with Mr Rankin. I missed them but I knew that was a better home for them.

We came here to Coober Pedy first and we were looking round for opals for a little while.

Roy Smith and his family was here. And he said, 'I'm going to West Coast – Warramboo. Are you going to come – for a ride?'

'All right. I'll come.'

So two cars went down that way – two carloads. Roy Smith's family in the front and in our car – Kingkey's – Charmaine Welsh's mother and father; those two and my wife and I and Johnny, our first boy. Johnny was the only kid when we went down to the farm country, following Roy Smith. The farmers wanted some fences built there. So we done some fencing on that station.

Me and my wife would just go and camp out where I was cutting the posts. She had a tent, she was used to bush life. She was born at Mount Penrhyn. She used to just get a tub for washing, no washing machine. She used to go out for *kalta* – sleepy lizard – with her sister, Roy Smith's wife.

And while I was working on the fence, Roy Smith went back to Warramboo. That's the time I went down there – to Warramboo. That was getting close on Christmas time, so that was the time Glenys, the oldest daughter, was born at Wudinna Hospital.

We was doing odd jobs all around there like burning stumps and things like that and that's where I met some of the Lutherans, the bosses on those stations. They were mostly Germans on the stations this side of Minnippa. They'd ask me if I wanted to do this or that. I was working on a farm making a little paddock for one bloke and I was nearly finished and he must have been talking to another bloke – 'Oh, we need you for cutting posts,' or something like that. And I'd have to cut posts for the next person's fence, one thousand posts. A bloke named Ditersky.

It was different work from what I was used to in the station country. Once, I crutched some of the sheep. I was a bit more used to that part of it.

So we'd been there about five or six months – it was round about Easter time, when Glenys was a little baby, that we took off from Warramboo country. We decided that we'd go back to Coober Pedy.

◆Andamooka◆

After the West Coast, we was on our way back here but, instead of heading straight for Coober Pedy, we headed straight to Port Augusta way. We went to Andamooka – that way. That was the nearest from the West Coast.

We had enough money from the farm to see us through while we go somewhere else on the way home and we thought we might make a bit of money on the opal there. We had to work for a little to get the petrol price for the truck to come back here.

The kids were too young to go to school then, but later on, when the kids was a bit bigger, we went for the second time and sent them to school in Andamooka.

That's when I ran into Mickey Fatt and his family trying to get some Andamooka opal to go back with to Coober Pedy. 'Oh, jump in here! Dig around here in the area where I am.'

So I dug around. Found enough petrol price to come back to Coober Pedy then. Yes, we just stayed in Andamooka about a week. We wasn't in a hurry – just our own time we was taking. We had a look at Andamooka but I didn't like Andamooka much; I was more used to the Coober Pedy area so we came back because there was hardly any diggings here in those days.

◆Giving the Opal a Try◆

Back in the forties, just after the War, I used to come up here to Coober Pedy – Eight Mile or wherever the diggings was at the time. Or I used to come on the weekends and look around, just giving the opal a try. I might have a week's holiday from the station – it might be after a busy time like shearing. There were no bulldozer cuts at Eight Mile then. I was out there. It was all pick and shovel work. I used to go out and check the holes where they noodle.

All the old opal buyers around here, I used to know them all. There was an old bloke named Brady. He used to come here from Sydney; and an old bloke named Brown used to come from Sydney to buy opal. He had one of those T-Model Fords. He used to just come and go and take his time; no hurry in those days. He might have left his car in Adelaide and go back to Sydney by plane.

Then, when I got married, when we were on holidays from Ingomar, we used to come in on the weekends and look around; just giving the opal a try again. We'd come in for the opal – checking 'em out, finding out what we can. It used to be only shallow digging in those days – oh, about four feet or five feet below the ground might be the level where the opal might be lying.

I used to dig holes – about up to my chest; pick and shovel and chuck the dirt out. Oh, that was nothing. I was strong. My wife would come and she'd noodle what was on the dump. There might have been some chips I'd miss out from where I'm digging it. I'd chuck it up so they can look; only little dumps, the depth of the hole. My wife, you might as well say, she was born on the opal fields; at Mount Penrhyn, on the Ingomar road, thirty miles from the old station homestead. So my wife grew up with the opal.

In those early days, we used to just dig with our hands and we might have a little winch like the Big Winch on top of the hill here in Coober Pedy today. They call it a winch, but they used to call it a windlass. That's the real name for it. (A German bloke had that and he called it a winch.) A windlass just draws the dirt up. You've got a long still rope with an eight- to twelve-gallon bucket or light drum on the end, and you put it down the hole and put the dirt in it. Then the other bloke (you usually have a partner) would pull it up by winding the handle.

If it's heavy, there might be two blokes working on the windlass. They make it by tying the bucket on a piece of pipe, say like a two-inch or a three-inch-wide pipe. It sits there at the top of the hole and they wind the handle. When the bucket gets to the top, they just push the dirt out. They chuck it out on the ground to make it spread out a bit. Yes, they're working underneath and they've got another bloke working on the top or might be a couple of blokes – one's working the windlass, and then the other bloke is waiting with the wheelbarrow to push the dirt away from the top and make it spread out, to keep the dirt away from the hole.

◆Opal… Ohhh!◆

We stayed all around the Flats here at first – and at Potch Gully and German Gully. We stayed where we worked or stayed down the Flat. We'd just put our tent up or camp – we never had a house in those days. In the morning, we used to go to work. By ten o'clock, we'd have enough money; we'd have a handful of opal. We'd go and sell it to the old buyers. We had our own opal buyers around the place. Buy our tucker and that's all the work we'd do that day.

Later on, we worked out at Eight Mile (Geraghty Hill). On top of that hill, there was a lot of opal – straight there at Eight Mile. And that's where a lot of the blokes coming out from Italy went. And one company was really good. A mob of us used to be camping out at Eight Mile and we know they'll start early – about half past seven – and we'd be there, ready, waiting for them to chuck the dirt out – each morning.

He'd tell us to sit down in an area, and he'd keep chucking out. See, there might be three of us in this lot sitting down, and three in that lot. He comes out with the bucket of rubbish to chuck it away; the dirt, the sandstone, and usually there's some opal in it too. Nice, big opal – that big! And he'd chuck it out – to that side for the first mob. Next bucket coming up, they'd chuck it to the next one; different mobs, you know – all the people sitting around there. It was good, and that Eight Mile opal was really nice – red opals. And that was an eighty-feet shaft. In Eight Mile, it's fairly deep down to the opal.

We used to all live out there. That was before the school started here in Coober Pedy (1960). I only had one son and daughter, and they wasn't school age. There's not too many people around now that were there then. Not many left alive, or they went away. Mickey Fatt, Edna Williams' father, was there a lot. He might have been there when we were there. That's a stony place, Eight Mile. And when you go there today and find one of the camps we lived in in those days, you find that the opal is still good when you go out checking.

All the *A<u>n</u>angus*, all the Aboriginal people, used to work. When we was down in the Flat, and all those other little shallow places around here – Potch Gully and German Gully, Twelve Mile (Dora Gully), and Eleven Mile (Greek Gully) and at Eight Mile (Geraghty Hill) – we done a lot of work. Your own claim, you had to have.

And when we'd put our pegs up on our claim, nobody wouldn't even *think* of going into your claim. You can leave your pegs and shovel and pick, right there with your windlass, and you know nobody won't touch it. They were honest in those days.

If you found a place here, you might dig a hole first – just checking around like a prospector is how you might put it I suppose. You get *opal*! There! 'Ohhhh!'

You'd show those others – 'Oh, that's all right! Opal here!' They wouldn't come, they wouldn't worry. You'd let them dig somewhere near again.

Then if you thought, you know, you had a really good claim, you might pick that little bit of area – leave them have that other one. Yes, pick that area where you want to work. We know there'll be a lot opals on the Flat there. We don't mind sharing it. No, just get out enough money for our tucker, clothes, whatever we had to buy. Opal was so easy to get. It was a really nice size. It might weigh more than an ounce; might be four inches long and an inch wide. We'd get a handful; orange, green, red.

We'd save up. We always had a car after I sold my green truck.

◆Making a Claim◆

Another place we was living was down near the water tank. They call that the Jeweller's Shop area. I was working around there. That was another place where the opal was only shallow and easy to find. In those days, the mining claim area might be fifty yards. So we might have a hole here and, three foot away, we might put another hole. We'll put it six foot away and dig in this way.

You'd buy your miner's rights for twelve months. When you finish that, you pull the pegs out again if you don't think there's anything there, and peg somewhere else. You just take it to the Mines Department – go and tell them. And then they know where the land's been pegged out. They put it down in their papers and they'll rub out that claim that I had before. I'd pay again for the next claim; it might have been £10, I think. It might have been less than that; it might have been £5. (When you're registered these days, you've got to pay $100. It's not much if you have a find.)

You can work together with other people when you're pegging your claim – to help each other. You might have a company of four people. I might peg round on the front so that the others can have some ground so they can push the dirt on to it. Opal – just in an ordinary field, you know, doesn't run – doesn't spread everywhere. It just goes in one line. Say it's from the south-east to the north-east – it runs in one direction – then I might have pegged one side of my claim to keep other people away a bit.

The opal might run across a certain angle. They'll find which way the opal is running when they dig holes all around. They drill holes and on one side they might find no trace. So they'll keep drilling along where the opal is running. If you have a company, the other people can peg their claims all along. That'll be a fair bit. Some of the area might be fifty yards. So they'll have a fair bit of work down there – maybe twelve months work there.

We was only working about thirty-eight deep in the deepest part. See, it takes a long time to get down to the deepest depth because you have to make it so wide and not too steep; you have to go back so the bulldozer will fit in. Fifty yards is fairly wide. They might put a cut in half that wide. Then the next cut they put in will fill the other part of the claim.

◆Selling the Opal◆

In the early days, the people with the shop, like Mrs Wilson – they used to buy the opal. You could sell it straightaway. We might just sell our rubbish opal for food. The storekeepers would make money. Say I might have opal worth £300, but they reckon, 'Oh, that's about £100 worth.' Then they might sell it for £300. Well, they make £200 out of it. Everybody would try to make a bit of money; usually the opal digger gets out the worst.

But they were really good, those old opal buyers that came up here visiting – old Brady and Brown. We might keep a parcel for the buyers. They'd be home waiting, the buyers; they never used to go out. They had the little scales – they used to weigh it on the little scales. They'd have the little ounces in those scales; right down to pennyweights, they'd go – something no bigger than your smallest fingernail.

They'd look at those scales of theirs and they might say, 'Oh, that's so much.' It might be £200 or something. You'd agree to sell it to them. Sometimes you don't agree and you take it away. Not often. There's other old buyers around so you're not in a hurry to sell it quick.

Bob Trow was the first postman here in Coober Pedy at the underground post office on Post Office Hill Road. I got to know him. He'd weigh it and class it and he'd give the proper price for it. I used to go and see Vince Wake too. In the fifties and sixties, I sold Vince Wake quite a bit of opal. They weigh it. You might have red opal and you might have some green opal and they'll weigh it separate. See, the red ones're a lot dearer opals; in a different class, you know.

You might have three different lots. You might have some ounces of grey stuff and you might have an ounce of green ones and you might have an ounce or a few ounces of red ones; different types. And you might have shells – and that's why you keep the shells to one side. The round shells – you don't have to sell 'em; you might keep it till you get round about £30 or something like that. But these days, it'd be worth $1,000 one shell – a full shell, full of opal. They might be sea shells a long time ago but they turned into opal.

Then all the *A<u>n</u>angus*, Aboriginal people, had our own opal buyer when Pastor Traeger came. He was the first Lutheran minister for Coober Pedy and he'd come out to where we were working (might be Ten Mile, Eight Mile, anywhere). He'd buy our opal for money and sell us the food where we were living.

♦ The Bomb! ♦

They were still calling me back to the stations when they needed me and one time I came out to Ingomar to track ride their sheep. That afternoon it was getting late, so I pulled up at Cane Grass Swamp to camp. It was about four o'clock, I suppose. It was a nice sheltered place – a little bit of scrub there.

Next thing, I seen a big smoke going up west of there – Cane Grass Swamp. And I knew then that was the time of the bomb [one of the series of British nuclear tests, Emu/Maralinga 1953–57] – with the smoke going straight up in the air – I knew that was the bomb.

And after a while, wind sprung up strong from south – that evening. And the low wind wasn't blowing from the west – it was blowing south. And that smoke was out west from where I was. That would have been too far for the smoke to come across, because the wind was too strong from the south. It was heading towards Coober Pedy, the wind.

So I guess that smoke from the bottom area wouldn't have come where I was camped, but the smoke – you know the one that went up high in the air – that caught that top wind up high – the top wind that blows that wind. And it went straight over – directly over Cane Grass Swamp – right over where I was camped. And I heard jets flying up in there too, that evening. They was flying around – they must have been following the smoke that was going straight towards Maree from where the bomb went off – in that direction.

And that evening, as the smoke was going over, I could hear some little grit falling on the top of the canvas cover and over the Land Rover I was camping in – the big tray top. So I knew some little stones was falling out of that from the fallout. It was coming – that smoke was coming over the top.

When I saw the smoke go up – like in the pictures – I was directly south of Coober Pedy. I was between Lake Phillipson. We call it Cane Grass Swamp – near Robin's Rise.

The smoke was coming straight west. It wasn't as far as Mabel Creek west. I was going all the time out, so I don't know what the year was. Mr Rankin would have written it in the book but he's passed away a long time ago.

They call that top wind the prevailing wind, It keeps going all the time. Never mind where this bottom wind changes. You notice the high clouds. They travel this way all the time with the prevailing wind.

I had the camp sheet – yes, a big sheet over the top. When the little bits started falling, I thought, 'Oh, it's nothing much.' It was just stones. It might have been the fall out. It was from the fall out; the low smoke just went across going all directions.

The south wind was blowing up to Coober Pedy. But the top smoke – where that was going was east.

I know the jet was up there, following that smoke. So it was above my head. I never give it a thought but I know the bottom wind was blowing towards Coober Pedy heading towards Twelve Mile. It didn't come near me. It was coming across from the west to east. It was south. It was coming towards Eight Mile and Twelve Mile. I agree with them (Jessie Lennon and the others here in Coober Pedy) that the smoke came that way to where they were.

The smoke had to come to Mabel Creek and then Twelve Mile because that's straight in line where the bomb dropped. And Coober Pedy is a straight line in between.

That's only the one; the main one that I seen was the black smoke, not the one with the cloud, not the mushroom cloud. You see, the smoke was just like it was burnt – with rubber. Smoke was that thick – what I could see going up in the air. You can see straight down that area. I was on higher ground.

The high winds don't go any other way – they only go from west to east. Well, that's where the smoke was – up in that area – high.

I didn't talk about it much when I went back. I just said I'd just seen the bomb go off. We don't know how dangerous it was. We just said it and forgot about it. We knew they were letting bombs off. They had jet planes up there, flying around, following the smoke.

Later, after I finished working on the station, I came back to Coober Pedy to live, following bulldozers and mining with the miners. They employed me as a checker – in the back, walking behind 'dozers.

I knew a lot of those blokes passed away. Some people have talked to me about it – that it might have been from the bomb they passed away. Some of the 'dozers would have come just after the bomb went off. But the ground would be where the fallout was. When they 'dozed the ground, ripped the ground up, the dust was coming up, out of the ground. Might have been poisonous.

My wife passed away through cancer. I don't know what that's through; it might be smoking. Died not very long ago, about four or five years ago. I never thought of that – the bomb. I thought of cigarettes – she had it in the throat.

I didn't get any of that smoke where I was parked. It was only the high smoke that went past. The bottom smoke must have blowed across, go across to Coober Pedy – because the wind was blowing that way. The top wind goes from the west.

L to R: Don Tanner, Billy Brown, Alf Turner, Mrs Hann, Ivy Lang and Ida Lang at Mabel Creek Station, c. 1947. 'Alf Turner – he's the one who came down and took me out from the Home.' (Photo courtesy of Len Beadell/DOSAA: Aboriginal Heritage SA.)

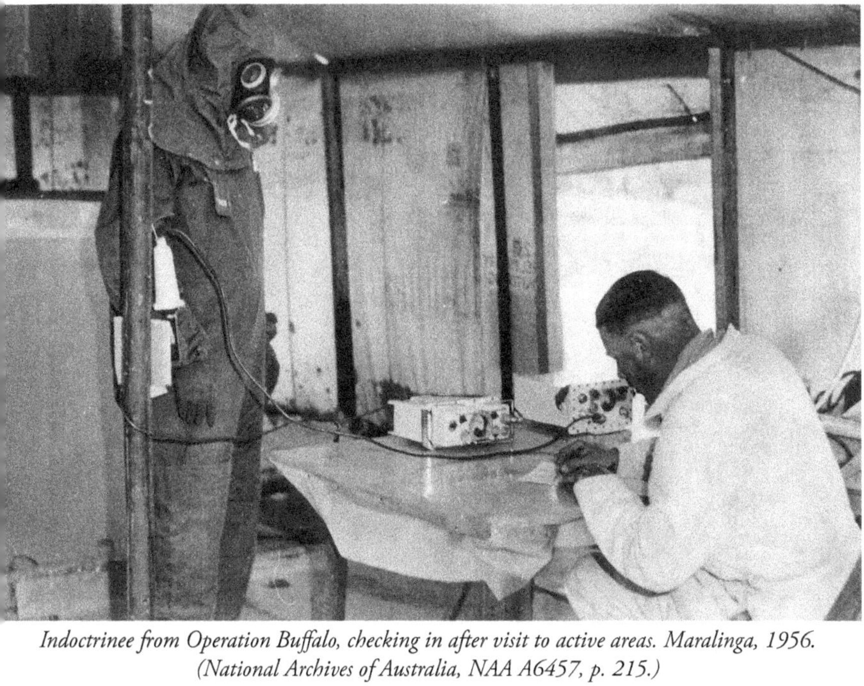

Indoctrinee from Operation Buffalo, checking in after visit to active areas. Maralinga, 1956. (National Archives of Australia, NAA A6457, p. 215.)

On an opal digging in Andamooka, 1947. Len Beadell, surveyor of Emu/Maralinga sites, is working the windlass. 'I knew Len Beadell. He w[as] always going up and down.' (Photo courtesy of Len Beadell/DOSAA: Aborigin[al] Heritage SA.)

Open-cut mining with bulldozer, Coober Pedy.
'When he [the miner] was pushing the dirt out with the bulldozer, I walked behind checking for opal.'
(Photo courtesy of the Traeger family.)

*L to R: Joan Russell, Jane Russell, Rita Dodd, Rosie Dodd, Sheila Gibbs.
(Photo courtesy of the Catholic Church, Coober Pedy.)*

*Umoona Reserve (now Umoona Community), established in 1959
with Pastor Fred Traeger as the administrator. These tin houses were demolished in 1999.
(Photo courtesy of the Traeger family.)*

Roy Smith, taking Umoona kids to school, 1960s.
'We travelled with Roy Smith and his family to Warramboo, a little place by Wudinna.'
(Photo courtesy of the Traeger family.)

The Shell direction sign, a well known former Coober Pedy landmark, 1960s.
(Photo courtesy of the Traeger family.)

*Coober Pedy, 1964. Brewster's Store is centre right.
Coro's first store is centre left, on either side of the main street.
The school (established 1960) is to the far left.
(Photo courtesy of Rhonda Traeger.)*

*Coober Pedy Lutheran Sunday School, with Pastor Eckermann visiting.
Pastor Grieger is at right.
(Photo courtesy of the Traeger family.)*

William Creek Races, 1975. L to R: Julie O'Toole, Glenys Dodd, Johnny Dodd, Pauline Williams. (Photo courtesy of Peter Caust.)

Jessie Lennon and Marty Dodd on an author's visit to Ingomar Station, 1997.

Three generations.
Back row L to R: grandsons Michael Dodd and Andrew Dodd with their mother Glenys Dodd.
Front row L to R: great-grandchildren Pamela, Beverly, Cynthia.

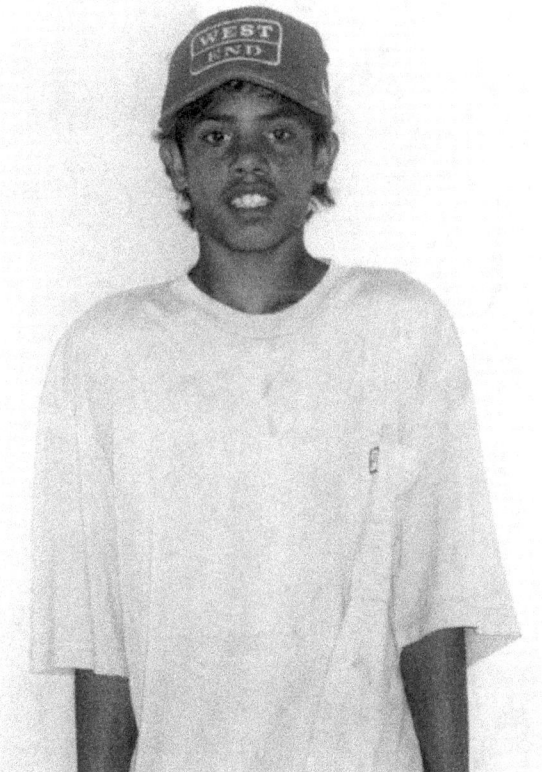

Steven Dodd, grandson, deceased Easter 2000, sadly missed.

*Marty Dodd with four of his adult children, Coober Pedy, 2000.
L to R: Christopher, Kevin, Glenys and Rosie. (Johnny, Robbie and Raelene absent.)*

*Marty Dodd with grandson Leslie
(Raelene's son) outside his new house,
Umoona, Coober Pedy, 2000.*

◆ Moving to Coober Pedy For Good ◆

For a few years, we went out again to Mabel Creek working, but we'd still come back weekends for the opal. Rankins had Mabel Creek – they bought up the different station so the sons would have something. White people were working there too – they had families there. And when they went away, they didn't have enough kids ready to go to school. So they let the school drop.

'Oh,' I told Mr Rankin, 'I might have to leave the station and take the kids to school.'

I was going to bring them back here to Coober Pedy. The two big ones, Johnny and Glenys, go in first. The other two, they were stopping home, Raelene and Kevin. I wanted to make sure they got their education. I got educated myself. It would help them in their later life. See, these people born out in Indulkana (Iwantja) and all that country, they don't worry about their kids for school; they don't care if they go to school or not. They didn't go to school themselves so they don't think about it. But, later on, times are going to change in every way; better for them if they went to school.

When I came into Coober Pedy to live this time, there were changes with the opal mining. They were getting into big machinery. They started drilling holes out from these fields. They might drill twenty or thirty foot down. They'd dig up holes sixty or a hundred feet. That's why they've got those fields way out there a bit – away from the town.

I only used to go back to the stations when they needed me. I had my kids going to school in Coober Pedy. Only when the bloke might want some mustering done, he used to come in from the station and ask me to go out for the week or month.

One of the times I was out at Mabel Creek, I was in the paddock towards what they call The Boxhole – out west of Mabel Creek, eighteen

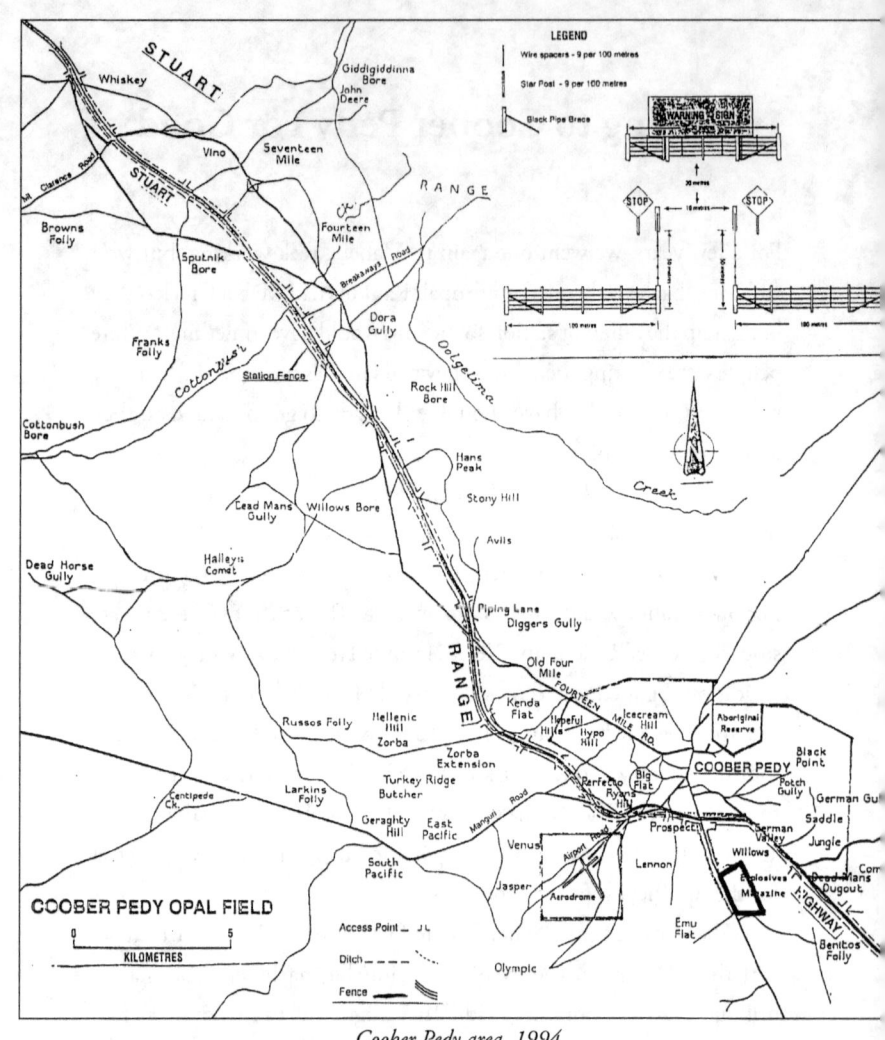

Coober Pedy area, 1994.
(Map used with permission of Primary Industries and Resources SA.)

miles out on the old Stuart Highway. That was when Bepi Coro's big store went up in smoke. I seen the smoke from there. Mabel Creek is twenty-eight mile out and The Boxhole – that's another ten or twelve miles the other side; nearly forty miles out I seen the smoke coming up!

It was probably shearing time. I was driving around the tracks to see whether the dingoes had got in, to check the bores and see the troughs were full. If there were any dingo tracks around, then I'd go and set the traps. One little kid, young Greg Rankin, used to go with me while I was driving round – for company. He's the boss of Ingomar station now.

I kept getting that work – they used to come and get me. Different people would come and ask, like Banjo Walkington, the overseer from Mabel Creek. I used to leave the family at home here in Coober Pedy out on the Flats or at the Jewellers Shop area near the water tank. Then afterwards I used to tell them I can't go if I was getting a little more opal 'cause one time I was digging a hole at one place at Seventeen Mile with a crowbar and, when I left it, there was opal at about two foot. I left it when Banjo came and picked me up. I only needed a couple more foot underground to run into the opal I was digging. Barney Lennon got £300 out of it and I didn't worry because I got the money that I wanted.

◆ The Bulldozers in Full Swing ◆

In the early days, it was just the pick and shovel and the windlass. Now the bulldozers were coming along and going deep. They dug down below the top levels that we used to pick and shovel work. They dug down between the top levels when they were working. So anyone might be able to find opal when you push some of it out from the high level – the alluvial level. Sometimes there's really good opal in there too. Well, that's what was happening when I came back here to Coober Pedy after I'd been working on the station for the last time (1975) – the bulldozers were in full swing.

Some of the blokes, the miners, found out that I used to work around the opal too, digging about. So they come and check up on me then and asked if I'd go and check for them – on a certain percentage. This is the job that checks behind the bulldozer driver. See, the man who ask me to work for him is paying for the diesel – oil, everything – so I only get a percentage, like a wage. They ask me how much I want – eight or ten per cent – and I might agree to that; eight out of a hundred, that'd be.

See, I was working down on the Flat there for a bloke called Ted; he's an Italian – Ted Commachio. I showed him the ground there. I knew someone that was working there, Billy Brown. Bobby and Daku live here today in Coober Pedy – their father and I knew he was getting a bit of opal there, hand digging. But too much level was there to dig it out. So I went and showed Ted that place and we dug there and I was getting eight per cent at that time.

When Ted went down about eight foot deep, the opal started coming up from the level ground – where the opal level is. And it was nice red and green opal. They got a fair bit, because I got £800 just for that day's work.

Sometimes you're not that lucky; you might work for a week or a month before you get anything – depends what depth you have to go. They would have got £8,000 or more. But I was just happy – it wasn't much work. I didn't have to work hard or dig for it. I was only walking behind, checking the opal, when he was pushing the dirt out with the bulldozer. I knew just about where the level was and I knew what level the other blokes got it there. That's only down at the Flat there. It wasn't very deep.

That opal was two foot, six and eight, ten and twelve foot below the ground around that area. The sandstone is in different layers. You might get a layer of dirt that's just nice – it makes the opal come in. There'll be opal in that area. That may already be about six feet. If you don't check it, you mightn't know it's there. It's hard to see – it's alluvial. Alluvial has dirt over the top of the opal and, when you throw it out, you think it's only grit and lumps of sandstone you're pushing out. But if you check carefully, you see pieces of opal sticking out.

Anybody that doesn't know – they can be checking behind the bulldozer and they think, 'Oh, there's nothing here.' Then they stand back in the corner waiting and the next thing – there'll be opal getting pushed out.

The driver might look down and say, 'Oh, there's opal in the ground here pushing out.'

And that's why you've got to check all the time, because you don't know when the opal will come.

No one knows where the opal is for sure. It mightn't be even at the level that the bulldozer is pushing out. It might be a vertical going down – a slide. It might start from up top and go down like that. You have to keep watching all the time then – because opals come out all the time. If anybody doesn't know, they might push it straight out – the opal. This is with the bulldozer doing the work.

Once they get a checker – if they reckon he's all right and good enough to check for them – they keep him as long as they can, you know. I used to work a long time for Ted Commachio. He's passed away now. He died of cancer – only about three years ago. He used to work here all the time in different places. We went out to Fourteen Mile way; I was working out there, checking for him.

When he got a lot of opal, about Christmas time, he'd had enough. He went away for a holiday and he might have went back to Italy. He didn't come back. He didn't want us to come back in the summer months. But we had to come back. About March, he'd come back. So I'd got a job with another bloke because we wouldn't have any money by that time. Yeah, I would wait for him as long as I could – but he never come back.

Yes, I was checking. Quite a few blokes I checked with like that. Bob McKenzie was the last bloke I checked for.

♦ Drills and Blowers on the Field ♦

There were a lot of people here in Coober Pedy then. That's the time when they were doing a lot – there was a lot of work going on; they were getting a fair bit of opal around. The ground was like new. They checked a lot of areas with a little drill to see if there was anything in that ground. Then they know how far the opal is. If they check it out and see little bits of chips coming out, they think, 'Oh, that's one level.'

The opal might be at twelve feet, something like that. So they'll keep going until they know what depth they might have to go down to check with the drill. Then they might say, 'Oh, this is a good area to put the bulldozer in.'

And they used to do that – put the bulldozer in. They might put three or four holes along there in the same line. That's the way to get the traces coming out in the drill holes. They put the bulldozer in there then.

The drill pulls the dirt out so you can see it. The drill just spins around – around and round and brings the dirt up. See, it brings the dirt up out of the hole and, whatever level it's going down, it's throwing the dirt up. When it's going down, the drill bit breaks the opal and the opal might come up. You see the chips coming up.

They've got big Cauldwell drills around for most of it now. You can see the big ones around because you have to go down deep nowadays, round about eighty foot in. In the earlier days, there were little small drills. But that's how they have to make a hole big enough to get inside these days. They just drill the hole and shaft coming up. They just stop the drill and work there and then and push the opal out. They've generally got another drill bigger to follow. See, the hole might only be a small size and they'd have another drill a bit bigger so they'd put the machine down.

Nowadays, you might go around the field, work around and see where the miners have been pushing their claims in. You'll see they got a big hole about four or five feet wide. They put the big machines – the blowers on the top all right – and they put the drill down that hole and that works inside. They blow shots of gelignite into the hole. Then they've got big pipes underneath connected to the blower and, when the blower starts, it sucks the dirt up. Different altogether from the pick and shovel days.

◆Bringing Up the Kids◆

Christopher, the youngest one, was only a couple of years old when the wife left me. After that, every day when I'm going for opal (I had to go for tucker money to feed the children), someone comes to look after the children while I'm out working.

That was all right, that part. I managed all the jobs – the kids were only small. I used to make sure I keep up to date with the washing – make sure they had clean clothes for the next day so they could go to school. I washed by hand in a tub, sometimes with a scrubbing board. If the clothes were a little bit dirty, I'd have hot water on the fire – heating the water first – no, no running hot water.

That just come as part of my life. I'd go to work at eight, eight-thirty in the morning. And I'd come back from work out on the opal fields at five or five-thirty. I'd be back in time to cook the supper and, if there were any dirty clothes, I'd wash that too – doing them nearly every day. That was the best way to keep them clean. Only need to make sure they don't get them too dirty. So it's best don't let them wear the clothes too long.

Mostly, the kids walked to school. Some of the time I was living on Umoona – on the reserve – living in a little humpy. Some of the time, when the bigger kids were young, I was living up near the big fan – the big windvane out where the power station is now. Up on the hill in the bushes camping there. No, we didn't have a house.

See, I had the three girls, Glenys, Raelene and Rosie, and one, two, three – yes, that's right – the four boys, Johnny, Kevin, Robbie and Christopher. Johnny was getting a bit bigger and before long he went away first but I had to keep going, keep at it, raising the kids till Christopher turned sixteen. I had to be there all the time while the kids were going to school – fifteen years without moving. That's how it was – very hard. But I took it in my stride. That's how life was, you know. I just took it like that.

It all happened when I used to go to work back to the stations when there wasn't much opal around here. I used to go out to Mabel Creek and work there – get some money for tucker for the kids, all the time. I think she got lonely then.

We were talking about it, before, me and my wife – that she might go one day – that we might split up and she might go somewhere.

'Yeah, that'll be all right,' I said. It's all right for her to go if she want to go. But the worst one was when she want to leave all the kids! I said, 'You can't do that. Really, the kids are yours. All these kids are yours. And you're suppose to look after these kids. A man – a man can go anywhere. He doesn't worry about his own children. Plenty of men leave their wives and the wives look after their kids – right through to the end.' I said that to her.

'No, I've already signed the kids over in your name.'

'Oh, well, if you don't mind it, that's all right, then,' I told her.

Otherwise, if she had've went with the kids, I would have packed up and went to Queensland somewhere – somewhere a long way from here.

But when she said, 'No, I've signed your name at the welfare office – I've put the kids down in your name...'

She shouldn't have done that! She should have waited till I came back and then talked to me about it, about signing the kids over. Oh, we might have had a bit of a talk, but I still think I would have agreed. I never thought she would have done that. I thought she would have taken her kids with her – or whatever kids she liked. But she just dumped the lot – you know, she didn't worry about them.

But I knew the kids like me – like me better – all the time. Bringing all the food home for them, I suppose – all the time. I wasn't really shocked, because we'd talked about it. Some people have fights and split up. But we never had a fight. We just talked to one another and made the arrangements. So everything was all right.

When you think – you know, rationally – there's no need to fight!

There's no need to have a big argument or anything. I just tell her, 'Oh, you just go your way if you like, if you don't want to stop. We're not tied to one another. We're married to one another but if you don't want to stay – you can make life somewhere else.'

She said to me before she went, 'Oh, you're too old for me anyway.' But she didn't know she was going to die before me – a long way before me. She thought she'd live young all her life. She was in a lot of pain – especially with cancer, something like that. She smoked like a train – smoked all the time. She went thin. The sickness – it come on her quickly, you know. She had a pain in her chest – it must have built up quick inside her.

She went away – Alice Springs way for a good while – a fair while. And she come back when she was getting sick, I think. She thought about her family then. Come back. She was living in a couple of houses – with Rosie, then with Glenys and Raelene. Some of the grandchildren were around by then – the bigger ones – Andrew, Trevor and Charmaine. She died of throat cancer.

Yes, I grew up those kids from when she left. I just had to be there all the time all those years till Christopher was sixteen. And then Dick Nunn, the manager of Anna Creek Station, came into Coober Pedy for the races. And when I asked him, he said, 'Yes, I'll take him on.' Nearly all the kids went to Anna Creek some of the time working. The girls Raelene and Rosie were stock workers too. They rode a horse too. Glenys was in the house helping the cook. I went across to see Johnny and Glenys who went there first, and then Christopher worked there. Kevie worked there too for a while, and Robbie worked there too, but he got hurt there one day when a horse stepped on his foot. So he come back here. Christopher grew up there the rest of his young life with Dick Nunn at Anna Creek Station. He was one of the main stockmen.

After Christopher left, I was free, a little bit freer. I'd had fifteen years growing them up in between going for opal. I was father and mother. And today they're all back here in Coober Pedy with my grandchildren. Yes, I know all my grandchildren, I know them all. I don't worry about counting them – I know them by their names. I don't know how many I have. I don't count them, they're around all the time. They won't go away from you. They've not gone away, really, only one. The oldest son Johnny lives a long way at Utopia – the other side of Alice Springs. He came back for Christmas. And he came for a funeral here the other day, but I missed him. I had to go to Port Augusta to hospital that day. But he left one, the girl – the daughter. Stopped the granddaughter. She wanted to see me. Karen. I just kept her here till school was starting – that September holidays. She stopped here till near the end of the holidays and we jumped on the bus. I took her up Alice Springs. And I rang up and Johnny came in to meet us and take her. It's about 130 kilometres. They were just ready to go back then. They were keen, and school started that next day.

Sometimes I go up there to stay for a while. Yes, my father came from up that way. But this is my home, Coober Pedy. Everybody who's been here in the community for a long time knows me.

◆I Know the Area That Much◆

I know the area that much – from Andamooka to Mintabie – all the country. I know the opal and I know the rock holes too, all the ones that are off the road. On that old Alice Springs road that used to go through before the bitumen come in, the road used to come round past Mabel Creek station and we used to go to a place called Box Hole. That's on Mount Willoughby Station country now. And we'd come to that big rockhole called Malu Kapi – Kangaroo Drinking Water.

And, along a bit further on, there's another couple more rock holes down the side of the road. Nobody don't know that now, 'cause they haven't been on that road – these young people. I can go there straight away today if I had to – to that place where the rock hole is. I haven't showed that to anybody.

I know where the burial site for my wife's grandmother is; that's just off the main road now. It's in Mount Clarence country. The grandmother was helping shepherding the sheep in those days when there was no paddocks around – that was before all the paddocks got put in; that was a good while. That was before I married my wife, 'cause I was still at Mabel Creek at the time. So they've been round here a fair while, the Lang family.

Yes, we *Anangus* was here – have been round here all the time. Other people that say there were no Aboriginal people around here in the early days don't know, because they only just come here lately! I've been here seventy years now, I suppose, just about. See, I'm seventy-eight. When that army truck went through that time with the Americans that were stationed up there in Alice Springs – that was way back in the forties – and I'd already been here six or seven years.

At the Jeweller's Shop area, near the water tank, there were a lot of people there. Some of them went down to Yalata way after. There was an old bloke called Doonga – Julie, his daughter, was only a little kid then. They came from up this way – Michael Dodd and all them. They were living in those places down there – Yalata – but they really came from up this way. If you get into Ceduna and look around, you still know a lot of people there. I know a lot of people there – they come in from Yalata.

I used to know a lot of people by sight – Frank Findlay from Ooldea used to come over this way from Kingoonya way; he was working on stations around that way...

They were moving around up here before they let those bombs off – before the 1950s. A lot of the young people don't know this. The Old People used to keep coming back. See, a lot of those Ooldea people used to go past Ingomar – when they used to travel on foot all the time from Ooldea. They used to go through that place – Cane Grass Swamp. They'd go down to Bushman's Bore and go through to that railway siding the other side of Tarcoola – Malbuma; they'd go back on business. These blokes used to come up here – they'd have a business meeting. They'd just go the shorter distance – go straight.

A lot of them used to camp out Potch Gully way. We used to camp out that way. Those people used to walk a long way. Strong people, and not much grog was around in those days. Kenny Smith's grandmother is buried there at Tarcoola. They used to bury them where they died. They couldn't carry them. There was only walking. My father-in-law's father, he was buried in Lake Phillipson too – old Frank Lang. People would know where they were buried. (Two girls from Amata came up to me just yesterday and said they were still looking after *my* father's grave.)

There use to be a lot of people – a lot of *Anangus* – at Kingoonya Races. And they all disappeared. Lot of them passed away. They used to come in for the races.

Up this way, there was no battles or anything like that in the old days with the whitefellas. This part was quite all right, mainly because we was all independent – get our own opal, and go and sell it to the buyer. See, we had our tucker all the time. We knew where our tucker was coming from the next day. We had a lot of claims everywhere; never even pegged it. No one wouldn't even think of touching it.

It's only sometimes a fella – A<u>n</u>angu, Aboriginal bloke – might go off the job from a station and they used to get the policeman to go and pick 'em up and take 'em back to work. Sometimes, people weren't really free like that.

Sometimes, things might happen between the miners. There was one bloke out here at Nine Mile going north towards the Twelve Mile diggings; someone was missing there once. He was getting ready to go to Queensland. He had a little car and a motorbike. The car was still there but the motorbike and everything was missing from his house when everybody looked. So somebody did bump him off, I think – just to get his money and opal off him. They knew a good claim was there so he must have made a bit of money and that was why he was ready to go to Queensland. But he didn't make it.

But that didn't happen much in the early days. Before the bulldozers and a bit after they came in, the miners were really good people, ordinary working people. It's only when the new people came out in the later times that it started getting a bit rougher. But they'd never go near a poor bloke – never go near somebody like us. They'd only look for a rich claim.

I never had prejudice from the miners. I used to work among all sorts of miners – Italians, Yugoslavs. I was one of those that worked. I mightn't have a big deep claim – but I had a shallow claim.

◆Epilogue◆

Yes, I'm still pretty fit, just a bit of trouble sometimes with my eyes. I still go out with my grown-up girls, noodling almost every day. That's all they know – they were brought up with the noodling and they're pretty good at it too. It's their trade. They can find the opal chips where a normal person can't find 'em. I'm a little bit hard finding it but they can just pick it up and have a bottleful in no time.

I'm still with my kids a lot. We might go out to a different field – Eight Mile or Four Mile or Ten Mile, somewhere like that – any place where there's been digging we might go to. Find something.

The noodling machines have come in and made it tougher – that's true. But we still noodle. We still go out. We still know where the old dumps are. Long years ago, when they were only little kids, they know the dumps. They say now, today, 'We know this place – dump when we were little kids.' And they see underneath the old dump, the opal, still good underneath – that's been away from the sun. It's still in dirt underneath, it's still as good as it was when it come out of the ground. But if it lies in the sun – it's no good. Even if it's really close to the surface, it's still no good, because in the summer time the sun gets really hot and might crack it.

My daughters still tell their friends where the dumps are when they find something – when they find some opal. They don't tell any strangers that have come here recently. They go out together. That's how it is.

My daughters go out with other friends like Lulu O'Toole they've known all their life. They've got friends like the other ones born here and grow up in Coober Pedy – they've been noodling all their lives. They know one another all their lives – they were sitting on their mothers' laps and mothers noodle. My wife used to love to go for opal. That photo of her on the dump is probably at Eight Mile.

Yes, I had many years with the opal – checking behind the bulldozers, working for this one and that one. Digging it out before that and later on again, noodling on the dumps. Like I am still here today, noodling.

But what I really am – is a stockman.

Appendix 1
Timeline

c. 1890	Tommy Dodd, Marty's father, is born in the Northern Territory.
1914–18	World War I – the Father trains horses for the army.
1921	Marty is born at Todmorden Station.
c. 1926	Marty's mother dies in child birth; he and his brothers are removed to Colebrook Home, Quorn.
c. 1934	Marty goes to work at Mabel Creek Station; his horses race at Kingoonya.
1939	The Flood.
1939–45	World War II; Marty meets American soldiers.
1945	Marty goes to Ingomar Station; his horses win Kingoonya Cups.
1948–49	Marty's horses win Oodnadatta Cups.
1953	British nuclear bomb tests (later known as the 'black mist') at Emu.
1956–57	British nuclear bomb tests at Maralinga.
1956	Marty marries Rita Lang.
1957	Marty's first son, Johnny, is born.
1959	Marty goes to the West Coast of SA; his daughter Glenys is born; he tries opal.
c. 1964	Marty's family move into Coober Pedy; his children attend school.
1970	Tommy Dodd receives British Empire Medal.
1970s	Marty checks for opal behind bulldozers; he does occasional station work.
1973	Marty raises his family while working the opal fields.
1975	Fire at Opal Inn. Marty finishes with station work.
1987	Christopher, youngest of Marty's seven children, leaves home.
1990s	Marty becomes involved in cultural sites and land protection work.
1996	Work begins on *They liked me, the horses, straightaway*.
1999	Marty becomes chairperson of Umoona Aged Care Aboriginal Corporation, and a member of the Executive Committee of the State Elders Council.

Appendix 2
From the *Australian Dictionary of Biography*

DODD, TOMMY (c.1890–1975), stockman and cameleer, was born about 1890 at Running Waters on Henbury station, by the Finke River in the Northern Territory, about 75 miles (120 km) south-west of Alice Springs. He was one of several men of shared Aboriginal and non-Aboriginal ancestry who bore this name in that era, and his life was typical of many of his people. His father was of Afghan and European descent, and came from the Hergott Springs (Marree) region of South Australia. His mother was a Pitjantjatjara woman from a group which, in the early 1900s, had been absorbed by their north-east neighbours the Matutjara. Tommy was born in a bush camp and raised among the Yankunytjatjara in the Everard Ranges.

A competent horseman by the age of 10, Dodd was taken by a station-owner to ride in bush meetings. He gained a reputation throughout Central Australia as a horsebreaker and broke remounts for the Indian Army. He was short and wiry, and his gait in later life reflected his years in the saddle: bowed legs and a limp resulting from the many fractures he had received. In remote areas in the north of South Australia he worked at mustering, horse-breaking, yard-building and fencing on stations such as Todmorden, Mount Barry, Granite Downs, Wallatina and Everard Park. He drove supply-carrying teams of camels from Oodnadatta to Alice Springs, then travelled west into the Aboriginal reserve to trade food for dingo scalps – obtained by the Pitjantjatjara and Yankunytjatjara people – on which the government paid a bounty. During these expeditions he gained knowledge of a vast area of the country and learned much about the mythological and ritual life of the Aborigines. A Pitjantjatjara woman recounted that, as a girl, she had been surprised to see him dancing with the men in a ceremony.

His first wife Rosie was an Arrernte woman. Their four sons were sent as youngsters to the Colebrook Home for Aboriginal Children at Quorn, South Australia, and their parents had limited contact with them. Dodd had two other wives from Pitjantjatjara Yankunytjatjara country, Katie Tjungura and Tjunyun, as well as another son and daughter. He spent periods at Ernabella mission (established 1937) in the Musgrave Ranges where he assisted the staff as an interpreter. In the 1950s he lived at Ernabella, before moving west to the Amata government settlement after 1961. In his old age he received a state pension.

Dodd's familiarity with Aboriginal life prepared him for his role as guide, informant and interpreter for government officials, patrol officers and researchers. In 1963 and 1966 he acted as a translator for the ethnologist Norman Tindale when he recorded Pitjantjatjara ceremonies. Dodd accompanied officers on their patrols to protect Aborigines in the area of the Woomera Rocket Range; for this work he was awarded the British Empire Medal in 1970. The *Advertiser* described him as 'a quiet, decent fellow who knows the NorthWest better than any other man'. Survived by at least two of his sons, he died at Amata Hospital on 22 January 1975 and was buried in the local cemetery. His gravestone is inscribed: 'A man of two worlds – stockman, camelman, guide and friend'.

N.B. Tindale, *Aboriginal Tribes of Australia* (Canb, 1974); W.M. Hilliard, *The People in Between* (Adel, 1976); *Advertiser* (Adel), 13 June 1970, 4 June 1971; information from Messrs B. Evans, Plympton Sth, Adel, M. Dodd, Coober Pedy, R. Trudinger, Ernabella, SA, R. Verburgt, Kuranda, Qld, and Mrs A. Elliott, Teesdale, Vic.

W.H. EDWARDS

Taken with permission from page 14, *Australian Dictionary of Biography*, Volume 14: 1940–1980. Di–Kel. Edited by John Ritchie. Melbourne University Press, 1996.

Appendix 3
From *The Adelaide Chronicle*, 1956

Boundary Riding Is Now Mechanised

By John Maher

Between the stockman's wide-brimmed hat and high-heeled leather boots there's a motor bike these days where the horse used to be.

On sheep and cattle stations throughout South Australia and the Northern Territory motorisation is replacing the horse.

Some stations still use horses for driving sheep to the railheads, but most mustering these days is by motor cycle or Jeep.

Three stockmen on motor cycles recently drove 3,000 sheep 80 miles from McDouall Peak station to the railhead at Kingoonya in outback South Australia.

Something seemed to be missing as the sheep gathered around the watering place — no horses, not even sheep dogs.

Head stockmen, in charge of the droving, was half-caste Martin Dodd; the other 20th century stockmen were Don Campbell and Adrian Alston.

Martin Dodd, 32, and one of the most respected and reliable half-caste workers in the north-west of Australia, said in his deep cultured voice: "Well, the horse is on the way out.

"The motor bike is quicker when you've got hundreds and sometimes thousands of square miles to cover mustering sheep.

"If they are well looked after the motor bikes stand up to hard wear. But when we are droving the bikes are no quicker than the horse — our speed is governed by the sheep. We usually cover 10 miles a day.

"We don't use sheep dogs — it's easy rounding up the strays on the bike. We'd just have to carry the dogs on behind," Martin added.

Mr. Glenn Rankin, of Igomar Station, where Martin is employed, said: "Our sheep are afraid of horses these days — but they don't take any notice of the motor bikes.

"Stockmen aren't the horsemen they used to be — station methods have changed greatly in recent years."

Mr. Rankin, his father, and two brothers own four stations covering 4,000 square miles.

His graceful station home has air conditioning and a green front lawn, kept green by bore water in a red, brown and grey land.

A young man, Mr. Glenn Rankin, believes modern methods are the best.

"But even though the horses are going, the wide-brimmed hats and the stockman's boots won't change," he said.

(Courtesy of Marie Nourse [née O'Leary].)

Appendix 4
British Nuclear Bomb Testing in South Australia 1953–1963

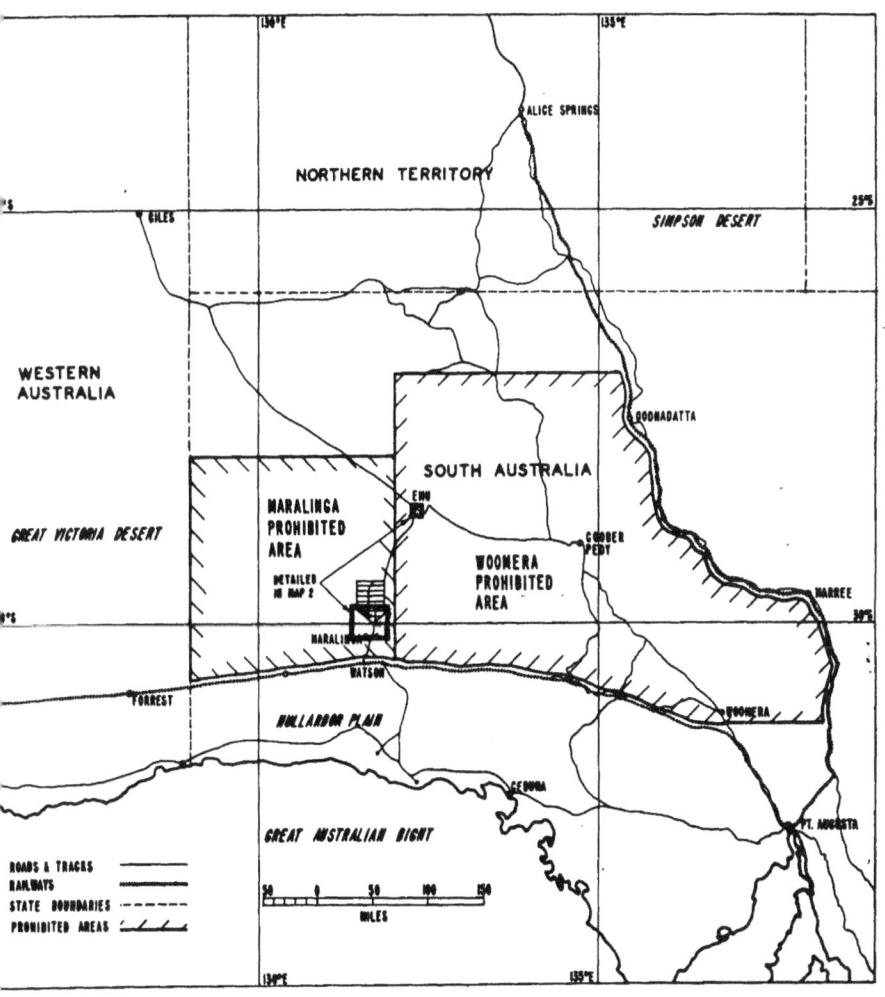

Two bombs, Totem 1 and 2, were detonated at Emu in 1953, seven at Maralinga in 1956–57. The so-called 'minor trials' involving plutonium took place up till 1963. Note the extent of the Woomera Prohibited Area. (From National Archives of Australia NAA A6456, R120/126.)

PRIME MINISTER'S DEPARTMENT.

ADMcK:NM

~~TOP SECRET~~ AB 29/5/85

M.143.

The Prime Minister :

You will recall that I mentioned to you in Melbourne the possibility of making a public announcement about "Totem".

Further consideration has led us to believe that it would be better to delay making any such announcement for some time and for that reason we have not proposed it to the United Kingdom. Our reasons are :-

(1) Without prompting, the United Kingdom have informed us that they hope to keep the operation secret for a considerable time;

(2) Woomera is an excellent cover to the activities associated with Totem and it is not thought that any speculation will arise for some time;

(3) It would not be wise to make the announcement until such time as we had cleared with the United Kingdom the whole question of publicity policy; we do not want the local press until we are in a position to tell them just why they can't be there.

I am attaching a letter from Mr. Cockram addressed to yourself. There are only one or two points which call for comment :-

(a) I assume you will want to establish the principle that any announcement should be agreed jointly between the two Governments; and   *Yes*

(b) At the suggestion of Professor Titterton, we intend to put to the United Kingdom that an Australian with Australian assistants should be made responsible for a particular segment of the intimate part of the operation. This would, of necessity, be quite small involving only about 5 personnel. It has two advantages -

(i) We commence to gather a small nucleus of Australians with intimate technical knowledge of the weapon; and

(ii) If this test is the first of a series, then Australia will be associated with them in some capacity other than that of "hewers of wood and drawers of water", whatever their atomic counterparts may be.   *Yes Ran*

We are getting comments from General Stevens on the more detailed matters raised in Mr. Cockram's letter.

[signature]
for (A. S. Brown)
Secretary.

5/3/53

Prime Minister Menzies' responses are written to the left of the text.
(From National Archives of Australia NAA A6456/3, R065/004.)

COPY

TOP SECRET

TELEPRINTER

ML 3404

EXTOT 130 - TOP SECRET

TO: ELMHIRST

FROM: STEVENS

PLEASE PASS THE FOLLOWING TO PENNEY FROM MARTIN AS SOON AS POSSIBLE.

REFERENCE YOUR TOP SECRET LETTER OF 5TH MAY 1953. IS 15000 FEET ABSOLUTE MAXIMUM. OUR BALLOON FLIGHTS FOR 1951 AND 1952 DISCLOSE WINDS AT 30000 to 40000 FEET OF UP TO 100 KNOTS WITH EASTERLY AND NORTH EASTERLY COMPONENT IN OCTOBER. WORRIED ABOUT MELBOURNE IN EVENT OF UNEXPECTED LOCAL RAIN. IMMEDIATE REPLY REQUESTED AS POSSIBLE NECESSITY FOR AN EARLY ANNOUNCEMENT.

See Marty Dodd's observations on page 69 regarding high prevailing winds. (From National Archives of Australia NAA A6456/3, R065/005.)

TOP SECRET ATOMIC GUARD

File No. 6012.1.154   19th February, 1957.

ATOMIC WEAPONS TESTS SAFETY COMMITTEE

Report to the Prime Minister on the Buffalo Trials
Maralinga - 27th September and 4th, 11th and 22nd
October, 1956.

SUMMARY

Four atomic weapons were fired in the series, the first and last (on towers) being of approximately "nominal" bomb yield, the second (at ground level) and third (air drop) being of much smaller yield.

Stringent safety conditions were imposed for the firing of all weapons and detonation only occurred after those Safety Committee members on the spot had, together with their United Kingdom colleagues, arrived at a considered opinion that no dangerous effects would arise in the Commonwealth or in the seas around.

Measurements of ground fall-out and air contamination were made at 86 monitoring stations throughout the Commonwealth, while rain water samples were monitored and mud samples from reservoirs were tested for radioactivity. In addition, certain tests were carried out on sheep to confirm that no untoward biological effects had occurred.

After a careful analysis of all these data the Safety Committee has satisfaction in reporting to you that the safety measures taken were entirely successful and there was absolutely no risk to any individual, livestock or property at any time during the series of tests.

L.H. MARTIN
W.A.S. BUTEMENT
E.W. TITTERTON
L.J. DWYER
D.J. STEVENS

(From National Archives of Australia NAA A6456, R075/004.)

www.ingramcontent.com/pod-product-compliance
Lightning Source LLC
Chambersburg PA
CBHW070930080526
44589CB00013B/1456